Values in Conflict

Edward W. Wheatley, Ph.D., holds an undergraduate degree from Fairleigh Dickinson University and graduate degrees from the Wharton Graduate School of Finance and Commerce, University of Pennsylvania, and The Florida State University. His business experience includes market research, advertising, and marketing management. He remains active as a consultant to business, and is the author of over twenty published monographs and articles in the fields of marketing and higher education for business. He is currently preparing, as coauthor, a text in marketing management.

Contemporary Issues in Business and Society

by Edward W. Wheatley

Banyan Books
Miami, Florida

For
Sara & Richard Bozarth
Chief Executive Officers, R. A. Bozarth, Inc.
and
Walter Beran
Partner, Ernst & Ernst
for their example

HD
60
.W47

Copyright © 1976 by
Edward W. Wheatley

Library of Congress Cataloging in Publication Data
Wheatley, Edward W. 1936-
   Values in Conflict
   Contemporary issues in business and society.

   1. Industry--Social aspects. I. Title.
HD60.W47   301.5'1   76-6097
ISBN 0-916224-05-8

Designed by Bernard Lipsky

Manufactured in the United States of America

No part may be reproduced in any form without permission in writing from the publisher except by a reviewer who wishes to quote brief passages for the purposes of a review.

Contents

Preface vii
Acknowledgments ix

1 **Business, Individual, and Social Change** *1*

The Seventies—Prologue to Business and Social Change/What is This Book's Objective?/What Are You Worth As An Individual?/How Should You Proceed?

2 **Human Values—Their Role in Business Issues and Decisions** *8*

Values Defined/Are Values the Same As Beliefs?/Beliefs—A Matter of Degree/Basic Sources of Controversy and Conflict/How do Values Affect Your Attitudes, Beliefs, and Behavior?/The Values of Business/Generalizing About Business: A Word of Caution/Is Business a Profession?/What Values Are Most Important to the Businessman?/An Approach to Conflict Resolution/Discussion Questions/Suggested Class Projects/Supplementary Readings

3 **The Young Consumer—Advertising and Children** *25*

An Issue That is Part of a Problem Packaged in a Dilemma/What Is the Effect of Advertising?/Advertising—Good or Bad?/TV Advertising and Children—The Setting/What Does the Advertiser Get for His Millions?/What Are the Effects of TV Advertising on Adolescents?/Should TV Advertising to Children Be Banned? Yes!/Should TV Advertising to Children Be Banned? No!/What Would Happen If Children's TV Advertising Were Banned?/Postscript/Discussion Questions/Suggested Class Projects/Supplementary Readings

4 **Energy Versus Ecology—The Santa Barbara Blowout** *49*

The Event/The Remaining Events/Get Oil Out? Yes!/Clean Up Methods—A Tragic Comedy/Get Oil Out? No!/Oil's Ecological Effect—Major or Minor?/Santa Barbara, Part of a Bigger Issue/Postscript/Discussion Question/Suggested Class Projects/Supplementary Readings

5 **The Unplanned Yet Inevitable Purchase** *75*

Unexpected Yet Inevitable/Mandatory Buyers of Unsought Goods/

Meet Roy Winston/The Traditional Funeral, Culture, and the Consumer/Discussion Questions/Suggested Class Projects/ Supplementary Readings

6 Women's Role in Business *86*

Why Was Phyllis Rejected?/Discrimination in Business/Vive la Différence/Women's Place/Stereotypes—The Language of Discrimination/Stereotypes and Sex Typing—Characteristics and Examples/Women in Management—Objectives and Responses/ What Do Men Want?/The Law—New Ally for Women in Business?/The ERA—A Final Answer?/Women at Work in Other Cultures/Is Business Really Serious About Women?/Discussion Questions/Suggested Class Projects)Supplementary Readings

7 Man Versus Mangroves *111*

Development—Its Dimensions/Development—Is Bigger Better?/ Coral Gables—Paradise of Prosperity/Paradise in Peril?/The Battle Lines Are Drawn/The Plot Thickens/Cocoplum Development Plan—Down But Not Out/Cocoplum—Yes!/Developers Submit New Plan/Cocoplum—No!/A Continuing Postscript/Discussion Questions/Suggested Class Projects/Supplemental Readings

8 The Businessman's View of Social Responsibility *134*

Social Responsibility—Oversimplification in an Age of Great Complexity/Banking's Role in Social Action/How Can Businessmen Help—The Problem of Focus/Discussion Questions/Suggested Class Projects/Supplementary Readings

9 What Is the Business of Business? *147*

The Cycle of Controversy/Criticism of Business—Inevitable and Desirable/Business Criticism in Perspective/Business Critics/The Democratic Paradox/Thesis of the Corporate Critics/The Tip of the Iceberg?/Criteria for Evaluation of Business/What Then is "The Business of Business"?/Discussion Questions/Suggested Class Projects/Supplementary Readings

10 Society and Business—What Does the Future Hold? *159*

Direct Pressures—Largely Due to Increase in Pluralistic Group Activity/Indirect Pressures/"Future Shock"—Will You Be a Victim or a Beneficiary?/Your Future/Supplementary Readings

Preface

In 1970 I became involved in studying the continuing critical dialogue between business and society. As the critique of business increased in scope and volume many teachers began to look for a way to integrate business issues into their courses. The number of "Business and Society" courses increased rapidly. Two types of texts developed: the major course text and the collection of readings. The major course texts, e.g., the excellent works by Steiner and Davis and Bloomstron, were geared to upper and graduate level business and society courses. Reading collections also appeared. They varied from somewhat structured attempts to mere aggregations of unrelated articles. The major course texts, while excellent for their intended use, were long, encyclopedic, and most appropriate for graduate courses in schools of business. Many readings collections lacked conceptual foundation and theme, leaving the instructor to provide conceptual themes and applications.

This book is designed to fill the current void. Its objectives are:

1. To provide students and teachers in a variety of courses at a variety of levels an opportunity to become involved in the current business and social issues debates.

2. To consider the impact of human values in the processes of business decision making and operations.

3. To provide basic data, sets of questions, projects, and readings so that new instructors as well as the professorial pro will find the text easy and fun to use.

4. To bring the heat of controversy and the light of informed opinion into the classroom for students' enjoyment and benefit.

5. To allow teachers to use the material to suit their own course needs whether the course be American Civilization, Introduction to Business, Business and Society, or some other.

To move toward the accomplishment of these objectives the book offers:

1. Reasonable reading requirements in both level and length.

2. Free standing chapters that may be used in sequence or in any other combination to meet instructor and course needs.

3. "Hot" case situations where sufficient data is presented to facilitate self-contained student analysis and discussion. Basic supplementary reading suggestions offer the student or instructor the option of a more detailed analysis. Group projects are also provided to generate class interaction and stimulate out-of-class activity. Project emphasis is on real-world involvement.

4. Issues are discussed from both sides of the question. Should society condone advertising to children? Both the yes and no positions and evidence are presented.

5. The issues are presented and positioned in such a way that the non-business, as well as the seasoned business teacher and student, will benefit from the material.

However the book is utilized, results will include an increased sensitivity to the importance and complexity of contemporary business and social issues. An inner appraisal of individual values and priorities should also occur.

Acknowledgments

I am indebted to many individuals and organizations for their assistance and support in the development of this book.

Thanks are due to George Steiner, Graduate School of Management, UCLA, and the General Electric Corporation for the challenge to participate in the "Contemporary Challenges in Business and Society" faculty seminar. This experience was the key motivating force for this effort.

The cooperation and encouragement of George Cubberly, John Dyer, John Stewart, and Charles Wurst, my colleagues in the University of Miami Department of Marketing, was a critical ingredient in making the project feasible.

Dan Steinhoff, Professor of Management, University of Miami, and Milt Blum, Professor of Psychology, Florida International University, drew on their experience as successful authors to provide valuable counsel.

Thoughtful reviewers at colleges and universities provided candid and constructive criticism that was integrated into the manuscript.

Barbara Goldstein, Kathleen Jones, and Paula Haston edited and typed the manuscript. Their suggestions, patience, and forgiving personalities helped move the work toward completion.

Hal Binford, former Business Division Chairman at Western State College of Colorado, and his faculty helped immeasurably by permitting a test of the unpublished manuscript in their business and society course.

At the University of Miami, Edward Fox, Dean, School of Business Administration, Nick Glaskowsky, Director of Graduate and Special Programs, Professors Edward Sofen (Politics and Public Affairs), Thor Bruce (Finance), and Manfred Ledford (Economics) provided varied teaching environments in which to test the manuscript. Archie McNeal, Director of Libraries, and particularly his research staff section provided facilities and services needed to make the task efficient and enjoyable.

The following individuals and organizations provided data and commentary that gave realism and the spark of honest debate to the issues: Fred Hartley, President, Union Oil; Crandell Jones, Standard Oil; Fletcher Byrom, Chairman of the Board, Koppers Company; Martin Stone, Chairman of the Board, Monogram Industries; Chauncey Medberry III, Chairman of the Board, Bank of America; Planning and Zoning Department, Coral Gables, Florida; Lisa Rose, *Miami Herald;* Alvin Weingand, Get

Oil Out; various operating and staff executives at Exxon USA's Houston, Texas corporate headquarters.

Finally, special thanks and love to Dody, Sarah, and Richard. They cheerfully accepted an uneven family routine and the sometimes uneven temperament of their family colleague.

1
Business, Individual, and Social Change

How will you relate to the business world of 1995? Of 2005? Will your involvement with business be satisfying or frustrating? Will what you have learned in the seventies see you safely through the next 30 years? Those of us who look smugly at the future, secure that our current knowledge will see us through, may be in for a shock. American society is changing. As our society changes so must the institutions that serve it. Those individuals and institutions which remain flexible and adapt to a changing society will survive and continue to perform useful functions. The American business institution is no exception to this Darwinian concept; neither are you or I.

The same concept applies to individuals. As the world around us changes we must change if we are to function effectively. The trick, for each of us, is to identify and defend those features of our business system worth preserving while remaining flexible enough to adapt to changing circumstances. If we can and do adapt, change will be a creative force. Change will stimulate, excite, and challenge. Change will be fun. If we cannot adapt, change will become a threat and an enemy.

Today the world of business faces several new and complicated forces for change. During the first half of the twentieth century business has adapted to significant changes. These include mass production technology, unionism, and government intervention. As the second half of the twentieth century unfolds social change is having its impact. The new issues involve ecology, growth, consumers' rights, business values, prejudices, and power. Modern American business faces new requirements and new social expectations.

This book is designed to stimulate you to think about some of the current pressures facing businesses and individuals in our changing society. Many of these pressures are based on the conflict between our value systems and our economic motivation for acquisition, growth, and profit — the problem of selflessness versus selfishness.

The Seventies — Prologue to Business and Social Change

Novelists and dramatists use the word "prologue" to describe the background information given to an audience prior to a dramatic performance. A prologue is like an overture preceding a concert. You may think that using the word "prologue" to set the tone for this book is a bit unusual; however, in the lives of businessmen, consumers, and public officials charged with regulating the competitive battleground of business the events that occur are often dramatic.

The prologue of social change is already being felt. The scope and pace of change are accelerating at an increasing rate. The vibrations of change are being felt in science, government, the arts, religion, the family, and in several aspects of individual behavior. Each of these changes carries important implications of our business system, a system which has been forged by an organizational and operational mode not always ready for change. For us to assume that business will continue to function unchanged through the indefinite future is folly. Business will change. The change may be evolutionary and internally motivated, revolutionary and externally motivated, or some combination of each. The question is no longer how business will change but rather in what ways the change will take place and how the changes will affect all of us.

Business will change because many consumers are presently dissatisfied with the gap between their expectations and realizations in their dealings with the business system. Business will change because the children of Aquarius bring somewhat different values to commercial transactions than did the children of the Great Depression. Business will change because the young students and executives of today will become the business policy makers of tomorrow. The newcomers appear to be more sensitive to the emerging social needs, the simpler human values, and the need to balance business power with business responsibility.

It is difficult to define how long the gap between society's expectations and realizations in its relationship with business has been at issue. It is even more difficult to clearly identify specific causes. What caused us to pause and begin to examine the business/society equation? Was it the threat of computerized impersonality? Was it the sheer size and political power of the business establishment? Was it the cumbersome inefficiency of government bureaucracies? Was it Ayn Rand, Vance Packard, Rachel Carson, John Kenneth Galbraith, Ralph Nader, Alvin Toffler? Was it the Kennedys, King, Bruce, McKuen, McCartney, Maynard, or Miles? Was it television, mass higher education, affluence, poverty, or ecology? Was it three wars in three decades or perhaps record levels of urbanization, mental disorders, alcoholism, drug abuse, violence, and crime? Was it a technology brilliantly conceived and applied to space vehicles, missiles, and nuclear weaponry while human problems begged for solution? Was it constant inflation and the business cycle? Was it foreign policy, the energy crisis, and the realization that, after all, perhaps the capacity of the earth has finite limits?

What Is This Book's Objective?

This book aims to prepare you for a changing business/social relationship. We have been teaching and learning about business in a relatively undisturbed atmosphere. Surely, there have been changes, but the changes have occurred within the existing structure. We have learned new and better ways to manage, market, control, and produce. Business principles and practices could be taught "by the book" with more or less standard questions and answers. As in learning to play classical guitar, you studied and practiced for years and then you went out and did it.

Well, modern business just isn't that simple. What business does often has significant effect on society, and what society does often has significant effect on business. Perceptive managers don't think of business and society as separate systems. Rather, business is part of our social structure and, in many respects, is a social science. Since society is changing, business must change. The purpose of this book is to impress upon you that business and its social relationships are open-ended, not closed; infinite, not finite; animate, not inanimate; and ever changing. I hope that you will develop the open-mindedness and flexibility to perceive, analyze, and deal with emerging business and social issues.

This book will bring you face to face with certain "hot" decision situations that reflect current business and social issues and the changing environment facing modern business executives. The situations presented in the following chapters will provide focus points for you to evaluate your personal position on topical issues involving the individual, society, and the world of business. More importantly, however, you will have an opportunity to develop a thoughtful response and an understanding concerning alternative points of view and action. In addition, you will enrich your own points of view by discussing the alternatives with colleagues, family, friends, or whatever other groups of individuals seem relevant.

In these days of mass controversy, mass selling, mass politics, overly simplified descriptions, stereotypes, and generalizations, you may be justifiably suspicious of this book. You may ask, does this book attempt to sell a viewpoint, social cure, or cause? Does this book damn business? Defend business? The answer, simply, is no. The book is primarily concerned with helping you focus on certain questions facing business, society, and the individual and helping you to develop the flexibility you will need to deal with complex issues and change. The problem situations are presented so that you can develop your own approach to feasible alternatives and tentative solutions.

You may rightfully ask, does the author have a thesis? Yes, I frankly admit to an incompletely defined and complex motivational set that compelled this effort. This thesis can best be summarized as "The individual is everything." The logical extension of this hypothesis is that if awareness concerning important and fundamental issues and questions can be intensified at the individual level, society will have an improved probability of success in developing satisfactory approaches in dealing with its problems. The more individuals involved, the higher the probability that the solutions will be of greater satisfaction to a larger number.

What Are You Worth As An Individual?

The evolution of human civilization is a story of change.

Dynamics of Social Change

1. Individual — independent generalist; strong personal value system.
2. Group — specialization; individual and group values.
3. Organization — combination of specialists; high organizational loyalty.
4. System — individual subordinated; system values supplant individual values except in personal life.

Each change has been motivated by the energy, the ideas, and the faith of individuals. As the process of civilization continues, the power and importance of the individual may be slowly but steadily supplanted by that of the group. Much of this change has been due to the concepts and efficiencies gained through specialization throughout every level of our society. As specialization and technology continue to fuel change and increase its rate of development, the group dynamic has become the organizational dynamic, and now we are drawing even closer to the possibility of unitary control in what may currently be described as the system dynamic. In business, for example, individuals and creative entrepreneurs have become combinations of specialists — the companies and firms. These organizations are then subsumed under a larger grouping of specialists — the corporation. Even corporations are being integrated or aggregated into "conglomerate" systems of business operations, and in a few industries, such as oil, we find the next possible step being one of unitary system action. This potential is so real that federal antitrust professionals monitor this tendency and attempt to provide countervailing forces to offset this natural process. This movement toward the system dynamic has not only affected business but has had similar effects on the family, education, government, and other nonprofit sectors of our economy as well.

The system dynamic has not been without major business and social benefits. It has permitted the technological base necessary for developing and accumulating the techniques to conquer the hostile aspects of our natural environment. It has resulted in an economic system producing the highest known standard of living and a government with enough muscle to defend and preserve the nation. There have been countless other benefits in the advancement of individual capabilities, individual freedom and opportunities, and a mantle of international leadership that has spurred continued advance and development. However, the system dynamic and the progress it has fathered have not been without costs.

Awareness of the potential imbalance between the costs of the system dynamic and the benefits is illustrated by the soul-searching questioning contained in the 1970 State of the Union Address: The time has come for a new quest — a quest not for a greater quantity of what we have, but for a new quality of life in America. In the next ten years we shall increase our wealth by fifty percent. The profound question is: Does this mean we will be fifty percent richer in the real sense, fifty percent better off, fifty percent happier? Or does it mean that in the year 1980, the President will look back on a decade in which seventy percent of our people lived in metropolitan areas choked with traffic, suffocated by smog, consuming poisoned water, deafened by noise, and terrorized by crime?

Our society's decision-making process has also become more complex. Today change often requires mass appeals, mass expenditures, mass promotion, mass production, mass communication, and mass participation. This last feature is a critical variable. As the mechanics of change become more complex, you may see your role in the process of change as less and less important and therefore pass the burden of evaluating and implementing the process of change on to smaller groups of special interest leaders. As a result, change is often less than complete, is usually indirect, can be untimely, and seems to be less satisfying. A shift in the base of power has also occurred. Critics of this power shift have been vocal in their condemnation of alleged misuse or nonuse of systemic power. The current power structure is often referred to as the "establishment." The "establishment" is the perceived current source of power.

Business is a wealthy, powerful, and important member of the establishment. This position of power is not only due to the resources under the direct ownership of business but also to the life systems its products support. These include our system of government and its subsystems supported through taxation, our social system supported by opportunities for labor, wages, and investment, and our life-styles modified by the changing symbols that business develops and markets. The inherent philosophy of business is efficiency, growth, and profitability. The continuance of a business organization necessarily means that it has successfully lived its philosophy, continued to accumulate power in its own right, and retained the power to influence the majority of its constituency. Critics of the business establishment often argue that this franchise for power carries in its contract an inherent and enforceable clause for social responsibility.

The future solutions to social issues involving business can be determined by the actions and influences of informed individuals. An important goal of the following chapters is to increase the probability that the basis of individual action will be carefully and thoughtfully conceived. In this book I hope to broaden the base of your concern, reflection, and communication. I hope that you will accept this challenge and participate vigorously in your own self-examination. If you do, your level of social consciousness will be elevated, and you can stimulate others to work for constructive improvement.

How Should You Proceed?

You should proceed with an open mind. At a recent conference devoted to understanding and improving the relationship between business, consumers, and government, the conference moderator made this opening statement: "We are hear to learn" (please note the spelling of the word "hear"). The moderator's introduction was indeed prophetic. He implored representatives from these three different, and not always friendly, societal subgroups to approach the conference with an open mind, to listen, to hear, and to learn. After a half-day struggle, this desirable attitude of open-mindedness was beginning to develop, and at the end of the three-day conference, a great deal of learning had indeed taken place. Representatives of business, consumers, and government were now in a better position to clarify issues, develop alternative solutions, and possibly implement satisfying and lasting change in seeking resolution of problem areas associated with the business-consumer-government interface.[1]

Approach the decision situations in this book with a fresh and uncluttered perspective. The following aids to clear thinking are suggested:

1. Read and reread each situation carefully. Define what you understand to be the major area of concern.

2. Develop the arguments and evidence that could be used to support both sides of the issues. Ask yourself if your prior background, knowledge, or biases cause you to identify more with one side of the question than the other. Honestly attempt to exchange roles. Strip yourself of your preconceptions and currently held points of view and place yourself squarely in the shoes of the other fellow. Analyze the problem from his point of view and attempt to understand his behavior and motivation.

---

[1]This conference was an activity of "The Program for the Study of Consumer Affairs." Further information concerning the Consumer Affairs conference and other plans and programs of this activity may be obtained by writing Dr. Milton L. Blum, Director, Program for the Study of Consumer Affairs, P.O. Box 8147, Department of Marketing, University of Miami, Coral Gables, Florida 33124.

3. Reach tentative conclusions. These conclusions should be your own, not necessarily ones in agreement with your colleagues or instructor. Identify the personal position that you believe in and would support.

4. Discuss the situations and your decisions with others. Beware of the trap of selective reinforcement. In discussing these situations with others, be careful that you have not consciously or subconsciously selected family members, fellow employees, fellow students, or friends whom you know will support your own point of view.

5. Remain objective and receptive to new information or changing conditions that could modify your point of view. Remember that "truth" is a relative term. Changing your mind for good reasons is a characteristic to be developed, not rejected.

6. As you complete this book, analyze your positions and their underlying evaluative criteria. Do you see any pattern evolving?

7. Finally, attempt to define the pattern of your responses, assuming you have given sufficient thought and consideration to all points of view, compared with your set of personal values. See if your response pattern is in concert with your own value system and the value systems of others. If you have never given concentrated thought to the development of a system of values or a philosophy the next chapter may help you examine this area more fully.

2

Human Values—Their Role in Business Issues and Decisions

At the bottom of all human activities are "values," the conviction that some things ought to be and others not.[1]

Why think about values? As you think about the problems and prospects of our society, you undoubtedly reach certain conclusions. In some instances, conclusions are based on accurate, factual knowledge. In other cases, conclusions are based on emotions, attitudes, and feelings. In most cases, conclusions are based on some combination of facts and feelings. In the next several chapters, you will be confronted with situations requiring you to render evaluative judgments and reach conclusions. Some facts will be presented but (deliberately) many will be missing. Through further investigation, you can and should add to the factual evidence developed in support of your conclusions. The depth of your feeling, the sincerity of your commitment, and the very perception of the facts themselves will depend largely on your own values.

If much of what you think, feel, and believe in depends on values it is essential to consider human values in attempting to understand the feelings and acts of individuals, groups, and organizations. The primary objective of this chapter is to cause you to look inward and examine your own emerging value system.

Values Defined

Definitions in the fields of values, ethics, and morals are often overlapping and somewhat unsatisfactory. One of the better definitions is offered as a case in point:

> Value is a word of wide and varied meaning. It may be used both in a positive and a negative sense; positive value will then be the good, negative value the evil. Good, in the language of daily life, is everything that directly or indirectly ministers to our needs or advances our welfare; evil, everything that opposes and thwarts our true interests.[2]

[1] Wolfgang Kohler, *The Place of Value in a World of Facts* (New York: Liveright Publishing Corp., 1938).

[2] Walter Goodnow Everett, *Moral Values* (New York: Henry Holt & Co., 1918), p. 36.

For our purposes, let's operate with the following definitions:
1. Values — basic beliefs used in the development of criteria for judging the worth of human conduct.
2. Ethics — the study of the criteria for good and bad conduct.
3. Morals — a body of principles of human conduct accepted by a society.

If you are to gain insight into your own evaluative judgments and understand those of others, you must first understand human values, value classification, and value sources. This may sound complex, but it isn't. What you really want to know is what type(s) of value(s) serve(s) as the foundation of my judgment or the judgments of others.

The ability to think and communicate clearly concerning values and value issues can have beneficial results in your life as a concerned and active citizen, parent, career person, friend, adversary, thinker, and leader.

Types of Human Values – Everett's Taxonomy

One of the first tasks facing anyone interested in studying a broad and complex subject is the job of classification. The benefits of classification and the resulting knowledge such activity provides is most evident in the sciences. People of scientific mind from all areas of inquiry have applied the process of classification with useful results. Classification improves communication as it provides each side with a clear basis for understanding the values related to the issues in question.

Walter Everett, a moral philosopher, developed such a classification for human values.[3] You can use Everett's taxonomy to identify the type of underlying value(s) affecting any issue under question. You can then move closer to the root causes of conflict, dispute, or even agreement, and then you can progress in your analysis quickly and directly.

Everett separated all human values into eight basic classifications: economic values, bodily values, values of recreation, values of association, character values, aesthetic values, intellectual values, and religious values.

Economic Values

Economic values are exchange values. Some economic goods have value because they provide direct need satisfaction. For example, the consumption of a taco has nutritional (and, for some, aesthetic) value. Other goods are valued for what they secure indirectly. Rather than direct values, these goods possess instrumental value. For example, a student's summer of hard physical toil as a member of a construction crew may

[3] Everett, pp. 182-223.

provide an income which can then be exchanged for other need satisfying goods and services such as a college degree. Thus, some things have economic value based mainly on their intrinsic properties, and others are valued primarily as being instrumental in securing satisfaction.

Economic activity often creates power. Economic power may be likened to the physical power of the atom. It can be used for good or evil, depending on the will of the users. Ideally, economic power should be used for the good of a society and its members. As you are aware, different societies have made different value judgments concerning the best type of economic system. An economic system is the method a society utilizes to allocate life's limited resources among competing and sometimes insatiable needs and desires.

Everett has his own thesis concerning the use of economic power (wealth):

> The ethical task is to moralize wealth ... all the processes of production, distribution and consumption must be recognized as human tasks to be dominated throughout by an intelligent moral purpose, not left to the impulses of selfish acquisition or to the unchartered exercise of natural powers.[4]

It is interesting to speculate that advocates of capitalistic and communistic economics could each make a case that their system satisfied Everett's criteria.

Bodily Values

Bodily values are based on the beauty of physical life. They include everything related to our health, physical presence, physical and mental well-being, and efficiency. Throughout recorded history it is possible to discern two basic and opposing sets of values relative to the body. Eastern philosophy and religion preached (and, ideally, practiced) asceticism. An ascetic is an individual concerned primarily with a life of thought and contemplation. Great self-discipline is practiced, and the pleasures of the flesh are subjugated to the purification of the mind and spirit. The body is viewed as a shell that serves as an early home for the spirit. Physical pleasures are shunned. Habits of eat, drink, dress, and recreation are austere.

The ancient Greeks and later the Romans championed the beauty, dignity, and worth of bodily values. Their cultures were filled with behavior based on physical conquest, competitive sport, recreation, and personal life-styles that glorified physical as well as mental well-being. Some historians have argued that the dissolution of the Roman Empire was

[4]Everett, p. 193.

partially due to a preoccupation with bodily values on the part of empire leaders and upper classes.

Today we face an intriguing and sometimes frustrating dilemma in situations relating to bodily values. Christianity and Judisim have established a somewhat ascetic approach to bodily values. Our society's moral codes are largely based on these two religions. And so our modern culture is in conflict with a moral code prescribing bodily restraint and an emerging national life-style based on increasing tolerance and individual freedom.

Values of Recreation

The basis of recreational values is the assumption that play is a pleasurable and useful activity for its own sake. An individual who opposes human conduct based on the values of recreation is likely to present one of two basic arguments. One argument is that resources used for play could be better utilized toward some other more productive end. Such an argument demonstrates categorical opposition to the values of recreation. A less extreme position is that you may engage in recreation to the extent that the term is used in its most rigorous sense, i.e., "re-creation," which permits you to once again resume more valuable and productive activity. The so-called Protestant ethic embraces this second interpretation of recreation values. Man's primary good is achieved through self-sacrifice and labor. Man should be permitted his rest and recreation but only to the extent necessary to renew and refresh himself for further labor. The true value in recreation is the related result of increased productivity.

In any free association test, the word "play" will probably elicit a response of "work." Ideally, your work should be pleasurable enough to provide some intrinsic values of its own. Most of us can eventually achieve some measure of this ideal if we thoughtfully pursue this objective. In contemplating your own job or career, consider the following: "But work in all its more ideal forms, such as the creative activities of invention and commerce, of scholarship and art, is to a large extent pleasurable and so pays its own charges as it goes."[5]

Many members of our society seem to be riding a paranoiac pendulum sprung by conflicting feelings concerning work and recreation values. The Protestant ethic of our forefathers and parents confronts rising affluence, education, mobility, and a predicted leisure society in which work will be challenged as man's highest purpose.

Values of Association

These values have their basis in the world of human interaction. The first

[5]Everett, p. 197.

and perhaps the most important associative values are learned within the family relationship. Long after infancy and adolescence, family influences play a major role in associative relationships with nonfamily members. The family can have a profound and lasting effect on associative as well as other values. Associative values expand and change as an individual makes friends and forms a widening variety of associations, including those of school, social, civic, religious, political, work, and recreational groups.

Like economic values, associative values are values of exchange. They also have intrinsic and instrumental properties. For example, you receive very direct ego-need satisfaction when a valued friend praises you on the accomplishment of some difficult task. Simultaneously, your own associations with your family, community, and nation are instrumental in providing an environment for a secure and potentially productive existence.

Character Values

The definition of character values is based on a society's general agreement as to what type of human conduct is most desirous and virtuous. In our society these values recognize the desirability of tolerance, temperance, honesty, justice, love of fellow-man, etc. To the extent a society defines and practices just values of character, it will be assured, more or less, of a continued and secure existence. Some character values run counter to man's primal animalistic nature. It is perfectly natural for certain animals to abandon their offspring and for many fish to kill and devour their young, but such behavior is contrary to most human character value systems.

To ensure that civilization and the security of life it provides will endure, man strives to be civil to his fellows. While at any one time each of us may entertain a notion to engage in totally selfish, or perhaps even lawless, behavior, the impulse is normally checked by our character values. Without some generally agreed-upon guidelines to individual conduct, human behavior would be governed by individual whim and opportunity. Under such conditions, no individual could long be secure; the civil environment would eventually give way to the law of the jungle. Without security the motivation for self-improvement and its corresponding rewards would lessen. Society would be in danger of sinking to its lowest common denominator.

Aesthetic Values

This group of human values is aptly summarized by Goethe's advice that each day you should listen to a little music, read a good poem, and enjoy the beauty of a fine painting. Beauty is the highest good on the aesthetic value scale. The aesthetic values of beauty can be found in both nature and in the works of man. Those who pursue their careers or avocations in the arts have a high level of awareness related to aesthetic values. Similarly, the outdoorsman, ecologist, and conservationist place high worth of the aesthetics of nature. Those who think and write about aesthetics generally maintain that aesthetic values must be cultivated through education and experience.

Intellectual Values

These are the values of knowledge in its widest application. These values are related to the activities of discovering new knowledge (research), examining and analyzing existing knowledge (scholarship), and the processes of disseminating and acquiring knowledge (teaching and learning). Critics of intellectual man often assume that intellectual activity must always be esoteric. Indeed, certain political figures of the 1960s and 1970s have painted a stereotype of intellectual man as cold, aloof, snobbish, and effete. In reality, it is seldom possible to separate feelings and emotions from intellect. The awakening of the intellect often comes through a specific interest and curiosity or a general desire to know and understand. Intellectual work is difficult and time-consuming. In such cases, it is usually the motivation and passion of the intellectual man that carries his work onward rather than the absence of passion.

The grist of the intellectual value mill is supplied by facts and theories. Intellectual man strives to define and describe things as they really are. He attempts to develop logical explanations based on consistant theory in cases where facts are not available.

Religious Values

Man's seemingly natural propensity toward religious values is eloquently expressed in the following statement:

> The values of religion, like all other values, are grounded in human nature ... Man is a religious being just as truly as he is an economic, or social, or intellectual being. Placed in a world whose mysteries transcend our knowledge, dependent upon forces which we can only very partially control, drawing our very life from cosmic processes and rendering it up again to them after a few short years, it is not strange that we all feel a profound interest in the nature of the universe in which we play our little part. Such interest is the very essence of religion.[6]

Review the writings and teachings of most religions and you will find codified behavior systems based on the religious interpretation of both

[6]Everett, p. 214.

worldly and spiritual values. The Ten Commandments represent one such religious value code familiar to most of us. Religions generally prescribe value codes that deal with man's conduct in life. Religious values are applied to a variety of situations, including self, family, friends, commerce, affairs of state, and man's relationship to nature and the spiritual world. For many, religious values represent a powerful force. There are at least three basic reasons for this. First, religion satisfies the need of man to relate to the universe. Second, religion is a well organized, long established, and respected social institution. Third, for many, religious education takes place during the formative early years of life and is often family-oriented. For most of us, religious education is probably the only structured and formal exposure to a value system we have experienced.

Are Values the Same As Beliefs?

You ask a friend, "What are values?"

Your friend answers, "Values are the things I believe in."

You argue with your father concerning the best way to pay for pollution control. Your father says, "I believe the consumer should pay for at least fifty percent of all pollution control costs."

You answer, "I believe that all costs to control pollution should be paid by the manufacturer responsible."

Certainly there is a relationship between beliefs and values. What you believe, however, is related to knowledge and perception as well as to values. Prior to addressing the issues presented in the following chapters, it will be useful to clarify certain distinctions between beliefs and values. The purpose of this discussion is to help you analyze what you mean when you say "I believe." Equally important is the development of your ability to evaluate the belief statements of others.

Beliefs — A Matter of Degree

In their persistent efforts to define reality, philosophers have carefully examined the concept of truth and belief. Aristotle was concerned with evaluating the truth of propositions raised in argument. He noted that controversy was based on representations of what people "believed" to be true. It became imperative to study the concept of belief in detail. Aristotle's analysis led him to hypothesize four degrees of belief. Arranged in descending order, these include:[7]

1. Certainty: Certainty is analogous to fact in the rigorous sense of the word. Certainty means that all evidence proves your belief to be accurate

[7]Karl E. Scheibe, *Beliefs and Values* (New York: Holt, Rinehart and Winston, 1970), p. 26.

and true. In matters of certainty, qualified observers would also confirm your belief statement.

2. Belief: The belief statement is based on all available evidence as perceived by the observer. At this level of belief, other observers may disagree and controversy may result. Probably most of our statements of belief are based on our own limited knowledge and perceptions.

3. Suspicion: Based on the detection of a few cues or even entirely on intuitive feelings we suspect something to be true. Suspicion is often based on the individual and unconfirmed biases of the observer. In the few cases where suspicion can be developed into total certainty, the observer becomes somewhat of a prophet. In most cases certainty turns out to be considerably different from suspicion when all the evidence is gathered and considered.

4. Doubt: Doubt implies a lack of sufficient evidence to form a suspicion or belief. The observer cannot become committed to a proposition at this point.

When someone tells you "I believe," you should clarify the degree of belief implied. As a minimum, be certain to evaluate your own belief statement as you prepare to assume positions on business and social issues.

Basic Sources of Controversy and Conflict

Differences of opinion concerning issues usually have their bases in the differences in the beliefs and values of the observers. Controversy in the business/society relationship is no exception. When you are involved in a dispute over differences in belief you have a higher probability of reaching a more swift and satisfactory conclusion than when the dispute is based on value differences. In cases where belief differences exist, you can often develop facts that will clarify the issue and lead to compromise and resolution. Where conflict is due primarily to value differences and the conflicting parties possess differing values or value priorities, successful resolution is less likely.

The following illustration is presented to clarify the difference between questions of belief and value. You can probably resolve an argument concerning the "belief questions" involving compact cars and the "Fortune 500 companies." The value questions are much tougher to resolve.

Question of Belief
1. What compact car has the shortest wet braking distance?
2. Which of Fortune's top 500 companies employs the fewest women executives?

Question of Value
1. Which compact car manufacturer gives the best service?
2. Is that company's practice justifiable?

How do Values Affect Your Attitudes, Beliefs, and Behavior?

Controversy and conflict in the business/society interface take shape in the form of confrontations between individuals representing, or sometimes claiming to represent, social and commercial interests. How are the attitudes, beliefs, and behavior of these individuals affected by their values?

The common denominator of nearly all of these people problems is to be found in the area of values. While it is commonly recognized that values differ widely from person to person and from culture to culture, their influence on people's thinking, acting, and behavior tends to be seriously underestimated. Their influence on the individual is powerful because:

(1) They principally determine what he regards as right, good, worthy, beautiful, ethical, and so forth (thus establishing his vocation and life goals and many of his motivations, for it may be assumed that he will seek that which he deems desirable).

(2) They also provide the standards and norms by which he guides his day-to-day behavior. (In this sense they constitute an integral part of his conscience.)

(3) They chiefly determine his attitudes toward the causes and issues (political, economic, social and industrial) with which he comes into contact daily.

(4) They exert a powerful influence on the kinds and types of persons with whom he can be personally compatible and the kinds of social activities in which he can engage.

(5) They largely determine which ideas, principles, and concepts he can accept, assimilate, remember, and transmit without distortion.

(6) They provide him with an almost unlimited number and variety of moral principles which can be employed to rationalize and justify any action he has taken or is contemplating. (If his stand is totally unrealistic, ludicrous, or even harmful, he can still defend it "on principle.")[8]

The Values of Business

If you accept the fact that "business" consists of organizations founded, staffed, and managed by individual human beings, the notion that business operates only on economic values will be considerably broadened. Like all human beings, business people play many different roles. An executive might be a parent, citizen, lover; a civic, political, social, recreational, and service group member; a student, musician, et cetera in the same week. In addition to a broad range of individual value inputs from business colleagues and customers, the executive's value system is conditioned by all of his life experiences. His values are based on experience occurring prior to his entering a business career, those currently taking place outside the business setting, and those which relate to the conduct of his current business affairs.

[8]Robert N. McMurray, "Conflicts in Human Values," *Harvard Business Review* (May-June, 1968), p. 131.

Each business decision usually involves a value input mix from several sources. Figure 1 illustrates this point.[9]

Business Decision Maker's Value Input Mix

Problem → Executive Decision Maker → Decision → Company Constituency (Employees, dealers, customers, etc.) → Industry → Society

Value Mix

1. Technical — facts and science
2. Economic — market values
3. Social — group and institutional needs
4. Psychological — needs of the individual
5. Political — general welfare of state
6. Aesthetic — what is beautiful
7. Ethical — what is right
8. Religious — theological beliefs

Fig. 1.

The value mix does not really represent a cohesive source of value inputs. Rather, value conflicts often exist within the individual's value system. In reaching a decision, the executive must balance value inputs. The executive is influenced in any one decision by a priority value ranking based upon personal values and the external circumstances relevant to that decision.

Generalizing About Business: A Word of Caution

"All generalizations are bad, including this one," said Voltaire. Certainly we must and we do generalize. In a detailed analysis of business/society issues, however, one must guard carefully against overgeneralization. When you say "society wants" or "this will be good for society," be sure to think about and be ready to specify what your use of the general term "society" means. The word "business" without further clarification also ranks low in its communicative voltage. The actions and options of an individual business are based on several interrelated characteristics. These include:

1. market served
2. product(s)
3. size
4. location
5. ownership
6. organization structure
7. age
8. industry structure
9. personnel
10. regulation
11. history
12. current success; future prospects
13. natural environment
14. technology

---

[9]The eight values listed were adapted from Keith Davis and Robert L. Bloomstrom, *Business, Society and Environment: Social Power and Social Response,* 2nd ed. (New York: McGraw-Hill, 1971), p. 135.

Before making a generalization concerning the actions of business and business executives, consider each of these characteristics and the effect they may have on the social situation of the company and the executives involved.

Is Business a Profession?

Is business a profession? No. Some professionals are businessmen and many business executives conduct their careers in a professional manner. But business is not a profession. A profession basically is any field of endeavor that satisfies the following requirements:

1. The activity is guided by a formal ethical code accepted by all members. Violators must answer to their peers for their actions and can be ejected from the profession.
2. The professional field is clearly defined and delimited.
3. Criteria for membership are established. These include educational experience and performance standards. Membership is then certified based upon meeting the prescribed criteria.
4. The basic motivation is service to humanity.

Examples of individuals commonly accepted as professionals include physicians, teachers, attorneys, engineers, ministers, certified public accountants, and career military. The term professional is also used in another sense, i.e., to designate any individual who receives money for his work or talent. Johnny Bench and Franco Harris are "professional" athletes. In that sense, Willie Sutton was also a professional. The dominant condition of professionalism is control. A profession, through its professional association, controls entrance, conduct, and expulsion. In considering these criteria for professional designation, it is easy to understand why business in general does not qualify as a professional calling in the full sense of the term.

Today, more than ever before in modern times, business is pursuing the goal of professionalization. In an age of sophisticated business competition, better informed consumers, a watchful government, and instant national communication, business is becoming more concerned with its long-run survival and social acceptance. Business is making advances in control (self-regulation) and the development of ethical codes. Control can be developed within trade associations as member companies increase their involvement, support, and commitment to their industry or specialization. Industries, companies, and groups of functional specialists are going on record with public statements of their ethical codes. George Steiner identifies three classifications of professional business codes:[10]

[10]George A. Steiner, *Business and Society* (New York: Random House, 1971), pp. 228-229.

1. **Company Creeds.** "... Company creeds or philosophies, which are usually short, widely distributed, and cover those basic philosophies that presumably govern the business ... There is no standard format for creeds. Some of them are fundamentally economic statements, but many are basically codes of ethics. Most creeds are written at high levels of abstraction and contain injunctions of the system of ethical standards..."

2. **Operational Policies.** These policies "... set up guidelines to action that have an ethical content. For instance, specific policy statements concerning such matters as procedures for hiring, promoting and firing employees; making decisions about dealers; or handling customer complaints. These policy statements are often rather detailed."

3. **Codes of Affiliate Organizations.** "... businessmen are members of clubs and other groups and are encouraged to follow codes laid down by these organizations." (Steiner notes especially the codes of trade associations and certain professions common in business, including accounting and engineering.)

What Values are Most Important to the Businessman?

You'll debate this question over and over. There is no final answer except "it depends." What is more important in the businessman's decision process — the values of our society that business serves, the values of the specific industry, the individual company, or the individual executive? The following chart is presented as a point of departure in dealing with this question.

Alternative Models for Business Decision Value Pressures

	Individual Model	Company Model	Industry Model	Social Model
Value Sources	Executive's personal value system	Company Executive	Industry Company Executive	Society Industry Company Executive

An Approach to Conflict Resolution

You have now examined several facets concerning the topic of values. You are now sensitized to the value and belief aspects of controversy and conflict. As you live the situations presented in the following chapters, you will be aware of their root causes — differences in beliefs and differences in values. As part of your own analysis of each situation and in evaluating the analysis of others, the following process will be useful. First, develop clear and concise problem statements. Second, separate the problems into two groups, those which are primarily due to value differences and those

Human Values 19

due to differences in belief. Third, for value-based problems, classify the nature of the value difference (use Everett's or some other taxonomy). Identify the probable sources and strengths of these values. For belief differences, identify key belief statements, related facts, and areas there there are gaps in evidence. Consider the sources and accuracy of beliefs as well as their strength (Aristotle's system). Develop a plan for conflict resolution based on value modification or compromise and/or belief modification due to improved evidence or evaluation. Finally, design a preventative early warning system that will reduce the likelihood of future conflicts or at least make recurring conflict more susceptible to early detection and resolution. Try not to overgeneralize.

The Conflict Resolution System Model summarizes the above process but is only one guide to problem analysis. You may wish to develop and utilize additional problem-solving approaches.

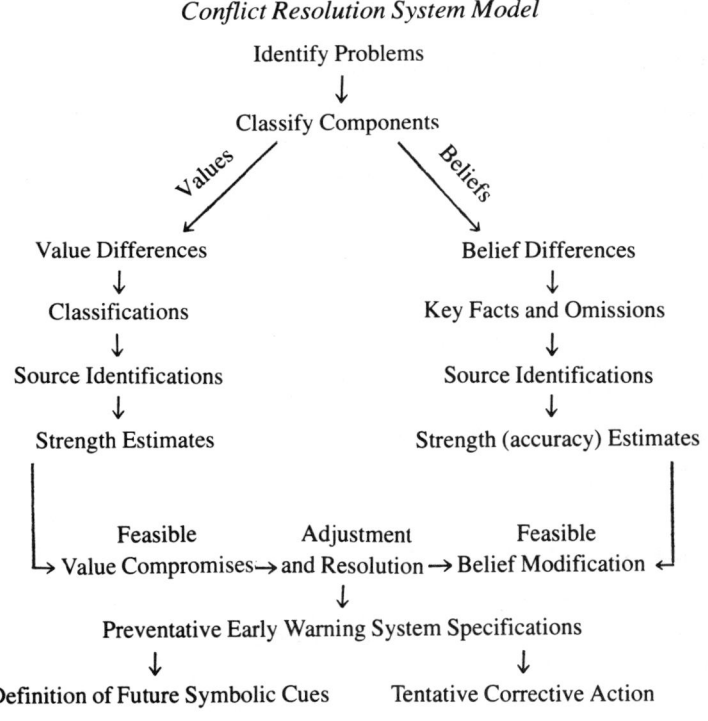

Fig. 2.

Discussion Questions

1. a. Define and compare "values," "ethics," and "morals."
   b. What role does each play in determining attitudes and behavior?
2. Using Everett's value system attempt to do the following:
   a. Identify those values that have the greatest recurring impact on your life.
   b. Rank your values in descending order of importance.
   c. Identify the source(s) of each value listed.
3. a. How often in the past have you taken time to consider your own value system?
   b. What are the reasons for the answer given in "a"?
4. a. Differentiate between questions of value and questions of belief.
   b. Why is it important to identify elements of conflict due to value differences from those due to differences in belief?
   c. What relationships do you see between values and beliefs?
5. Is Everett's system mutually exclusive? Discuss.
6. "Those looking for final answers and absolute truth may be dismayed when they understand the probabilistic nature of belief."
   a. Interpret this statement.
   b. How do you react?
7. a. Identify the sources of values in the "Business Decision Maker's Value Input Mix."
   b. Briefly describe each source.
   c. Develop and defend a value pressure ranking that you believe to be representative of the "typical" business decision maker.
8. "Business is bad." "Give a customer an inch of rope and he'll take a mile."
   a. What are generalizations?
   b. Do they aid or hinder discussion? Specifically, how?
   c. Is it possible to completely eliminate the process of generalizing from debate?
   d. What can be done to minimize communication problems caused by generalizations?
9. "In making an important decision, the individual executive is bombarded by an array of conflicting value pressures."
   a. Discuss the sources of executive value conflict.
   b. How would you resolve conflict in such a position?
10. Why is it important to have a structured approach to conflict resolution?
11. a. What changes in American values do you feel have occurred (or are occurring) during the twentieth century?
    b. What effects do you see resulting from the changes you have described?
12. a. Is business a profession? Why? Why not?
    b. If you feel business is not currently a professional field, do you feel it could become more professional? How?
    c. Would this be desirable? Identify at least one disadvantage.

Suggested Class Projects

1. A local manufacturing firm is under attack from a vocal and militant minority organization. The company did not appoint an apparently qualified minority group member to a recently created vice-presidency. Both the minority organization and

the company have agreed to submit this situation to you (or your group) for analysis and resolution.

   a. Develop alternative conflict resolution systems that could be applied to the analysis of the problem.

   b. What are the principal strengths and weaknesses associated with each of the systems you developed?

   c. In your judgment, what area of this conflict is likely to be most difficult to resolve? Why?

2. a. Write a hypothetical case situation involving business values and a major decision.

   b. Select three executives from the same industry or field in three different companies; meet with each executive. Have them read the case and ask them what decision they would make and why.

   c. Ask them to then identify which values in the "Business Decision Maker's Value Input Mix" influenced their hypothesis and in what way.

   d. Compare and contrast your findings.

   e. You may broaden your inquiry by interviewing executives from different industries, then contrasting responses by industry.

   f. Pose the same case situation to a student group. Contrast the differences in their reactions to those of business executives. What are some probable causes associated with these differences?

3. a. Arrange a panel discussion based on a comparison and contrast of the following books: Alvin Toffler's *Future Shock,* William Reich's *The Greening of America,* and John Kenneth Galbraith's *The New Industrial State*. The theme of the discussion should be "American Society and Institutions — A Study of Change."

   b. Allow 10 minutes for each panelist to summarize the assigned author's hypotheses.

   c. The moderator should then open the panel to the audience.

   d. Conclusions should be developed.

   This panel presentation will provide greatest benefit and interest when the audience is provided in advance with a synopsis of the three works being analyzed. Also, consider broadening the audience to include nongroup members from a wide variety of backgrounds.

4. "The influence of organized religion is stronger than ever before. The late 1970s and early 1980s will produce an upsurge in religious interest." "The influence of organized religion on American values is diminishing. This trend may create a value vacuum for the present generation of young Americans."

   Evaluate these statements on the basis of the following:

   a. Locate and analyze recent books and articles which discuss the issue.

   b. Secure official or officially sanctioned relevant reports from religious organizations.

   c. Interview clergymen from various denominations for their views.

   d. Interview teachers and scholars of religion.

   e. In light of the evidence collected, which statement appears to be more accurate?

   f. What are the implications of your conclusions?

5. a. Secure a recent copy of an ethical code for an industry, a company within that industry, and an area of specialization within the company. For example,

Industry: National Association of Appliance Manufacturers; Company: Tappan, Inc.; Specialty: Marketing (Ethical Code of the American Marketing Association).
b. Compare and contrast each.
c. Are the codes enforceable? Are they enforced? How?
d. What changes do you suggest?

Supplementary Readings

Books

Baumhart, Raymond C. *An Honest Profit.* New York: Holt, Rinehart and Winston, 1968.
Broad, C. D. *Five Types of Ethical Theory.* London: Routledge & Kegan Paul, 1956.
Bunting, J. Whitney, ed. *Ethics for Modern Business Practice.* New York: Prentice-Hall, 1953.
Clark, John W. *Religion and the Moral Standards of American Businessmen.* Cincinnati: South-Western Publishing, 1966.
Durant, Will. *The Story of Philosophy.* New York: Simon and Schuster, 1953.
Everett, Walter Goodnow. *Moral Values.* New York: Henry Holt and Co., 1918.
Garner, Richard T., and Rosen, Barnard. *Moral Philosophy.* New York: Macmillan, 1967.
Kohler, Wolfgang. *The Place of Values in a World of Facts.* New York: Liveright, 1938.
Margolis, Joseph. *Values and Conduct.* Oxford: Clarendon Press, 1971.
Maslow, Abraham H., ed. *New Knowledge in Human Values.* New York: Harper, 1959.
Sarbin, T. R.; Taft, R.; and Bailey, D. E. *Clinical Inferences and Cognitive Theory.* New York: Holt, Rinehart and Winston, 1960.
Scheibe, Karl E. *Beliefs and Values.* New York: Holt, Rinehart and Winston, 1970.
Selekman, Benjamin M. *A Moral Philosophy for Management.* New York: McGraw-Hill, 1959.
Walton, Clarence C. *Ethos and the Executive.* Englewood Cliffs, N.J.: Prentice-Hall, 1969.
Wylie, Philip. *An Essay on Morals.* New York: Holt, Rinehart and Winston, 1947.

Articles

Boulding, Kenneth. "Ethics and Business: An Economist's View." In *Marketing and Social Issues,* edited by Wish and Gamble, pp. 91-97. New York: John Wiley & Sons, 1971.
Carr, Albert Z. "Can an Executive Afford a Conscience?" *Harvard Business Review* (July-Aug. 1970): 91-97.
England, George W. "Personal Value Systems of American Managers." *Academy of Management Journal* 10 (1967): 53-68.
"Ethical Responsibilities of Labor." *Stanford Business Bulletin* 31 (1963): 62-69.
"Is Business Bluffing Ethical?" *Harvard Business Review* (Jan.-Feb. 1968): 143-146.
Keeney, B. C. "Bridge of Values." *Science,* July 1970, pp. 26-28.

Kennedy, John F. "A Statement on Business Ethics and a Call to Action." *Proceedings of a Business Ethics Advisory Council Meeting*. U.S. Department of Commerce, 1963.

McFerran, D. "Black Con III: The Black Value System." *Commonweal*, March 10, 1972, pp. 6-9.

McGuire, Joseph W. "Business and the Generation Gap." *California Management Review* (Winter 1970): 78-82.

McMurray, Robert N. "Conflicts in Human Values." *Harvard Business Review* (May-June 1963): 130-145.

Michener, J. A. "Revolution in Middle Class Values." *New York Times Magazine*, August 18, 1968, pp. 20-21.

Roths, L. E. "Helping Children to Clarify Values." *National Education Association Journal* (Oct. 1967): 12-15.

3

The Young Consumer– Advertising and Children

Enemy fire roars up from below. The artillery barrage misses, but machine gun bullets come searingly close to the lone figure clinging to the rope. Why is this single soldier the target of such deadly and concentrated enemy firepower?

After carefully infiltrating enemy lines, Sergeant Jim Jones, U.S. Army, was successful in photocopying the enemy's detailed plans for the coming invasion. While making good his escape, Jim's break-in was discovered. Every available man, gun, and machine was mobilized to cut off the sergeant's escape routes. Jim's speedboat awaits in the river at the base of the sheer cliff wall. An automatic winch carefully placed on the cliff's precipice unwinds the rope that lowers Jim closer and closer to his boat and freedom.

Suddenly the boat explodes, a direct hit from an enemy artillery cannon. Jim has one last chance — his contingency escape plan. The winch is activated, quickly bringing Jim back to the top of the cliff. Jim wastes no time in activating his emergency radio. The red light blinks — thank heaven the super-signal-sender-radio is still working.

Enemy soldiers are getting closer. Jim can hear their clamor as they ascend the slope leading to the cliff. Jim has no more ammunition. He unsheathes "Big Bertha," his famous combat knife, stands proudly, and awaits the enemy. Between the bursts of machine gun and cannon fire, designed to keep him pinned down for the kill, Jim hears the throbbing sound. It can only mean one thing — his desperate radio rescue signal has been received. Dropping from the clouds, a chopper gunship hovers over the cliff. Spraying rockets and 20 mm cannon fire, the chopper shuts down enemy gunners as it lowers a rescue sling. Jim is in the sling. Still hovering and spraying fire, the chopper crew winches Jim up. The chopper banks, streaks into the low hanging clouds, and within minutes its important cargo is safe behind American lines.

"G.I. Jim" combat set, $6.95, sold at all toy stores. Set includes Jim, Big Bertha, Jim's trusty rifle and pistol, and three combat uniforms. Other items are sold separately. Tell Mom to get you Jim today. What adventures you, your friends, and Jim will have!

You look at your spouse over Saturday morning coffee. "What a violent TV commercial," you lament, "almost as bad as the real thing." As you go back to your paper, the commercial is over and your kids' attention is drawn back to the tube. The interplanetary people have just obliterated the planet Zoftic with their deadly atomizer ray. The remainder of the cartoon will show how the lone Zoftic survivor, Luto, takes his revenge.

An Issue That is Part of a Problem Packaged in a Dilemma

The controversial business/society issue given most attention in this chapter is whether business should advertise to children. The decade of the 1970s is one of great uncertainty for both business and its critics in this topic area. The national focus created by the 1971 Federal Communications Commission hearings renewed the energies of business critics and sobered manufacturers and their advertising agencies. Before we consider each side of the television advertising to children issue, let's consider some of the larger questions of which this controversy is only a part:

1. Should children be subjected to any type of merchandise or service promotion? In addition to mass media advertising, marketers utilize other forms of promotion. Advertising is only one ingredient in the total promotion blend. Other ingredients include personal selling; sales promotions, e.g., various short-term, intensive efforts such as point-of-purchase displays, contests, sampling, premiums, etc.; publicity and public relations, for example, having a corporate trade character such as "Ronald McDonald" do public service work or speak at various schools. Creative packaging and attractive retail display work may also have some persuasive effect on young consumers.

2. What type of TV programming is best for children? Can commercials be considered the primary villain when program content itself may feature antisocial behavior, violence, murder, greed, and revenge? Even the mildest type of "baby-sitter show" can be condemned for not using its program content toward positive educational goals.

3. What about TV advertising to adults? What about advertising in general? Does it serve a useful function? If advertising were stopped or drastically curtailed, the issue of TV advertising would disappear. What are advertising's social and economic roles?

What Is the Effect of Advertising?

Picture the following events:
1. Bill walks into Fred's home;
2. Bill points a loaded revolver at Fred and pulls the trigger;
3. Fred falls to the floor, a bullet in his heart, dead.

Question:
What caused Fred's death?
Answer: Loss of blood? Stoppage of the flow of blood to the brain and other vital organs? Shock? The bullet? The revolver? Bill? The state's lax handgun laws?

Now assume that Fred had robbed Bill's dad's store the previous evening. Fred's elderly father had feebly resisted and was severely beaten by Fred. Bill's Dad had died that night.

Question: In light of this additional evidence, what would you say caused Fred's death?

Background question: What caused Fred to commit a crime that ended in violence? Perhaps those circumstances really caused Fred to die.

This line of questioning could be expanded indefinitely. The reason? We are dealing with the complex philosophical concept of causality. Why did an event occur? What caused it to happen? What was the true cause, the root cause?

How does the issue of causality relate to advertising? Business critics maintain that advertising causes people to want things they don't need, causes them to change their behavior, causes them to purchase. What are advertising's effects? No one really knows. What caused you to purchase a Ford Mustang rather than a Chevy Vega? Probably many related and hidden variables. Certainly advertising alone was not the single or even the primary cause for your decision.

We often have a somewhat confusing view of advertising. On the one hand we feel that advertising is an ultra-powerful force in changing consumer behavior. On the other hand, we are usually hard put to think of an instance where advertising caused us to purchase something we didn't want or need. Some inexperienced businessmen hold an equally simplistic view of advertising's effectiveness. This "push-button syndrome" goes something like this: "All I have to do to cause more sales is to spend more money on advertising — more advertising will cause more sales." Business executives and owners who know better may dream wishfully that competition was that simple and consumers that malleable, i.e., that any time a firm wanted more business all it had to do was push the advertising ("cause") button and more sales would occur.

Advertising research is in its infancy, and "experts" appear to disagree as often as they agree. However, one thing appears clear. Advertising has two main goals: to inform and to persuade.

As an information system, advertising comes under only mild critical fire. Informative advertising is classified as that which informs you concerning the introduction of new products and other functional and factual details concerning both new and existing products. These data include product description, performance specification, price, availability, variety, utilization, and competitive comparisons. The emphasis is on economic and functional data that you can use to evaluate competing products.

Persuasive advertising seeks to convince you that the product of the advertiser is to be preferred over competitive alternatives. The advertiser implies that the product is "best" for you. Sometimes persuasive advertising is based on claimed distinctive product advantages such as performance and cost. A Mazda television commercial that shows a Mazda RX3 winning a quarter-mile drag race over a Jaguar XJ6, a Mercedes 450 SL, and a Porsche 914 is one example. The Mazda is faster in the quarter mile and the advertiser reminds us that "you can have three Mazdas for the price of one Mercedes." This ad has economic (functional) and informative content as well as an appeal to your emotional and psychological side. More purely persuasive ads are the Schlitz beer commercials depicting he-men in action being independent, physical, and masculine. The ads say nothing about the product's functional attributes, cost, competitive differentiation, etc. The appeal is to one's psychological and emotional side. It says, "If you are a real man and live your life with gusto, you'll drink our beer" (if not you're a Caspar Milquetoast). Persuasive advertising is a primary target of business critics.

Advertising — Good or Bad?

Prior to zeroing in on the specifics relating to children's advertising, let's examine the typical criticisms leveled against advertising in general and typical defenses.[1]

1. Informational advertising is generally agreed to serve a useful social purpose. Classified advertising, local retail advertising, business paper advertising, and advertising that contains detailed information of an economic or functional nature helps you in product comparison and improves the quality of your decisions. Informational advertising has redeeming social benefit. There are, of course, gray areas in each category and in the definitional space between informative and persuasive advertising.

2. Advertising is inefficient. This argument is based on advertisers' inability to:

   a. Demonstrate the direct economic effect of the advertising expenditure, i.e., the ratio of return per dollar of advertising investment.

   b. Precisely identify target customers and beam advertising messages directly to them and them only. Advertising an expensive office copying system on a Barbra Streisand TV special with an estimated 25 million viewers is an excellent example. Probably only a minute fraction of 1% of

[1] Adapted from Jules Blackman, "Is Advertising Wasteful?" *Journal of Marketing* 32 (Jan., 1968) pp. 2-8.

the viewing audience have decision-making influence or capacity relative to brand selection in office copy machine purchases. Considering that time, talent, and production costs for an elaborate ninety-minute special can easily exceed $1,000,000, would it not be more efficient for the sponsor to use a qualified personal sales force to call on real prospects?

In response, the sponsor and agency involved in mass media advertising would cite the following counterarguments:

1. The scope of coverage could mean that many more prospects were simultaneously contacted than would be possible or economical through personal selling.
2. Prospects who were unknown, or who were not yet prospects but would in the near future become prospects, were reached.
3. Even though total costs were high, costs per prospect contact possibly were lower.
4. For noncurrent prospects and users of competitive products, a sponsor's prestige is enhanced by bringing such a show to the American television audience.
5. Of the 99-plus % of viewers like ourselves who will never be prospective system purchasers, some may become investors. National corporate visibility will enhance the image of corporate securities.
6. Public attitude will be favorable, furthering the probability that ongoing corporate public relations programs will succeed.

In summary, expensive mass advertising may be more rather than less effective than other alternatives, even when waste coverage is considered.

3. Wasteful competition results as companies seek to "get on the market" with similar products and expend large sums to shift demand between brands. The "democratic analogy" is often used to counter this criticism. A competitive market economy does produce duplication and waste, just as our democratic form of government is less efficient, in one sense of the term, than a dictatorship. Our great economic progress, however, has been based on accomplishments caused by the profit incentive freely applied to all who would compete. Without the incentive and relative freedom, a new and better life would not have been created. Even though duplication has its bad points, it does create employment and income for workers, managers, marketers, investors, and government.

4. Advertising adds unnecessarily to prices. The "volume defense" is most often used to counter. Where advertising increases sales volume, producers enjoy economies of scale. Unit prices are lower due to mass advertising and marketing.

5. Advertising creates useless needs. The advertising advocate would probably respond that your needs are innate, complex, dynamic, and a

product of many variables, advertising being only one. You bring your basic needs to the marketplace. The advertiser attempts to convince you that a particular brand will produce the desired need satisfaction. Advertising may have an interactive effect with needs, but advertising is not "the" cause of your needs.

6. Advertising corrupts values. In this argument, advertising is blamed for emphasis on material and economic values. And advertiser might respond by stating that advertising's role is indeed economic. A competitive economic system is an inseparable part of our society. If economic values and materialism are unduly emphasized by a society, the blame rests with the human value system of individuals, the family, and social institutions such as religion, education, and government.

7. Advertising creates artificial obsolescence, resulting in wasted resources. Defenders of advertising point out that there are three basic types of product obsolescence:

a. Technical obsolescence: in this case, a product is improved or even replaced by another more effective model. Replacement of the horse and buggy by the automobile is an example of technical obsolescence on a grand scale. The development of color TV, now in about 70% of homes with TV, is another. Redesigning or improving sound insulation to make an air conditioner run more quietly is a less dramatic but more common type of product modification that renders a new model more desirable than the old. Of course, better products and increased efficiency make older products look poor by comparison. Mass competitive advertising, however, is one constant stimulant for continued product improvement. New advances would not be made if everyone were satisfied with the status quo.

b. Fashion obsolescence: in this case products that still have economic and functional value are shelved or discarded in favor of "new" products. We want the new products primarily because of differences in their looks, not their functional performance. The annual model change in automobiles is an excellent example. You may want the new model when it is technically little different from present models except for its modified style. If the new style is accepted, it becomes fashionable for a time until styles change again. Clothing is another example. Narrow ties are supplanted by wide ties, straight pants by flare pants, pointed toes by square toes.

c. Mixed: here a new product has embodied both technical and fashion obsolescence simultaneously. This type of obsolescense occurs less frequently and appears to be somewhat accidental, i.e., the readiness of new technology concurrent with readiness on the part of consumers to accept a new fashion. The introduction of double-knit fabrics in menswear concurrent with the acceptance of pleatless flare pants and sport jackets with wide lapels serves as an example. Did men stop wearing their current clothing and switch to the new because they liked double-knit fabrics? Or, did they reject the older styles in favor of the new? Probably both variables were important, i.e., the double-knits felt great, fit well, and complemented the new styles in which they were featured.

Advertisers would probably defend product obsolescence using the following arguments:

1. Consumer needs: you desire change. You seek to express your individuality in many ways; the products you purchase is one method. You are a wanting animal. Your wants are both economic and emotional. As you change during your life cycle you desire new symbolic values as well as new utility from products. Business responds to these need complexities and dynamics. It does not create them.

2. Technological imperative: you desire to benefit from better methods and materials. Their discovery seems to be wasted if not applied to improvement in our standard of living.

3. Economic vitality: new products and product life cycles create jobs and income. New industries create economic growth and absorb into the work force aspiring young workers and future executives.

4. The competitive imperative: competition is based on difference, improvement, and change. In a market economy, if a company believes consumers want new fashions, new fashions will be introduced. If success results, other competitors are free to emulate and strive to gain a differential advantage.

5. The second market: in a free economy, several levels of economic strata develop. The $6,000 per year clerk cannot afford a new $6,000 car each year as can his company's $50,000 a year president. But the clerk can afford to purchase the same car three years later at $2,000. The "pre-owned" marketplace provides a complete variety of products from heavy construction equipment and computers to small appliances, furniture, and clothing. Products are available in a wide variety of price ranges and styles to suit almost any need.

Let's turn now from the general social complaints against advertising and common business responses to a very specific and more intense area of controversy — advertising to children. The most heated area in the battle over advertising to children is network television. TV requires no reading ability, no purchase cost to the child, and is primary occupier of children's waking hours. One method social critics use to impact broad existing social issues is to break the broad issue into smaller parts and attack each issue one part at a time. For the critic to be most effective, the sub-issue being attacked should have creditable content and emotional overtones. Advertising and children is an issue possessing both ingredients.

We will proceed by presenting research evidence relating to the question, "What are the effects of television advertising on children and adolescents?" You will then be asked to consider the arguments for and the arguments against the proposal to eliminate children's advertising from TV.

TV Advertising and Children — The Setting

Only in the past several years have people begun to question the effects of television advertising on children. I was a child when TV was first introduced into American homes. My reaction was like that of almost every other child I knew — we dashed home from school at 3:30 P.M., watched the end of the TV movie, and began our daily afternoon love affair with Howdy Doody and Buffalo Bob. From that day on, force was sometimes needed (and applied) to separate the first TV generation from its alter ego each night. Parents and kids alike were grateful for television and watched everything from programs to commercials (and even test patterns) with equal dedication. Ask anyone over 35 and you'll get the same story.

Today, television is part of our life-style. Programming has changed drastically to include expanded news, documentary, educational, and cultural offerings. Television regulation, both voluntary and imposed, has grown in volume and complexity. Discerning and well educated Americans are beginning to question and analyze the power of television, the press, and other mass media. Some parents limit their TV viewing and that of their children. A small minority of families have rejected TV and now spend family leisure time in other ways. America's television viewing families have become critics, selectively viewing only certain offerings.

It is impossible to accurately estimate the economic value of products consumed by children. Children consume many of the same products consumed by adults (food, transportation, services) and also influence the products purchased by adults for family use. That children represent an important television market segment is evidenced by statistics compiled by F.C.C. consultant Dr. Alan Pearce. The total gross revenue from weekend children's TV for the year 1970-71 was $74 million. This figure was up $5 million from 1969-70. Of that total, CBS grossed $40 million with an estimated $10 million profit. ABC calculated its profit at $7 million. NBC's profit was estimated at $4 million.[2]

What Does the Advertiser Get for His Millions?

What are the effects of television advertising on young children? In a study concerning children as consumers, researcher James McNeal carefully studied a sample of 72 children from four to ten years of age. This

[2] "Children's T.V.: Ethics and Economics," *America*, October 21, 1972, p. 309.

exploratory study produced some interesting tentative conclusions concerning children as consumers in general and children's attitudes toward advertising in particular.
1. With the exception of two respondents, children had a keen awareness of TV advertisements.
2. As the children studied increased in age, so did their dislike and distrust of TV advertising.
3. Indicative of the negative feelings held by older children in the sample were words like "untruthful," "annoying," "silly," and "repetitious." In addition, there was objection to the fact that commercials took too much time away from the programs.
4. Favorable attitudes were associated with entertaining ads, jingles, and cartoon advertising.
5. Over 50% of the sample themselves purchased or requested that their parents purchase many of the advertised items.
6. There appeared to be an inverse relationship between sample age and the desire to purchase goods featured in television advertising. By nine years of age 35% of the sample had a negative feeling concerning advertised goods. They believed ads exaggerated product quality.[3]
7. Girls developed scepticism toward TV advertising earlier than boys.[4]

In a prophetic remark, McNeal summarized his research report by stating:

> It can be seen from this study that today's youngsters become conscious of, and participate in, consumer behavior at an early age. Indications are that the significance of consumerism among children will become even greater in the near future.[5]

In 1965 William D. Wells, a psychologist who was also a consultant to Benton & Bowles Inc. (a large and well known advertising agency), released the results of an extensive research project. The detailed research results are far too lengthy to be reported here, but Wells concluded:

> Conversations with children produce six general observations about their influence on purchases, and their reactions to advertising on TV.
> 1. Children influence the consumption of products in several quite different ways — through personal purchases, through direct requests at home, through direct requests in the store, and through "passive dictation." A complete account of children's influence requires that all these ways be understood.
> 2. A major change in TV program preferences occurs between the ages of

---

[3]James V. McNeal, "Children as Consumers," Bureau of Business Research, University of Texas, Austin, 1964, pp. 21-22.
[4]McNeal, p. 28.
[5]McNeal, p. 28.

five and twelve but this change is not accompanied by a smiliar change in reactions to TV commercials. Tailoring commercials to specific age and sex groups is therefore less vital than it would be if reactions to commercials and reactions to programs changed in the same way.

3. Although children are ready to accept almost any premise, no matter how fantastic, they are alienated by unrealistic execution. In commercials directed to children, "believability" depends on child-defined "reality."

4. Some advertisers have done a much better job than others in creating commercials which advertise the brand rather than the product category. Some advertisers make children want their competitors' products as much as they make them want their own.

5. For attracting and holding children's attention, moving pictures are much better than still pictures and pictures of any kind are a lot better than words. Even though this principle is obvious, it is frequently violated in commercials directed to children.

6. Children are especially reactive to certain "motivating scenes" — scenes which announce an extrinsic reward for using the product, which feature genuine news about new products, which endow the product with magic power, which show someone wanting the product, which show someone enjoying the product and saying, "it's good," which demonstrate the product's attributes in motion.[6]

The National Institute of Mental Health funded several studies concerning the effects of TV advertising on children. The $25,000 grant restricted the size and scope of the work to exploratory research. The researchers are quick to point out the limitations of their work and describe their findings as tentative. Testimony concerning the results of this research was given before the Federal Trade Commission hearings on "Modern Advertising Practices" in November of 1971.[7]

The selected findings by Ward and his associates are summarized below. Three studies concerned TV advertising and young children, ages 5 to 12; three studies concerned adolescents.

1. Children's TV attention drops when commercials are shown. "Tuning out" is less among younger children and increased with age. About 60% of children under 10 years of age gave full attention to programming.

2. In only 12% of the cases did children's attention shift from partial attention to programming to full attention for commercials.

3. The research subjects made some comment concerning commercials viewed about 20% of the time:

   a. younger children commented mostly about the products

   b. 11-12 year olds comment equally about the advertised product and the commercial itself

[6]William D. Wells, "Communicating with Children," *Journal of Adventuring Research* 5 (1965), pp. 13-14.

[7]Scott Ward, "Effects of Television Advertising," *Marketing Science Institute Special Report,* Cambridge, Mass., 1971. Ward's report summarizes studies performed by him and several colleagues.

c. positive comments decrease with age; negative comments increase with age
4. Attention to commercials is functionally related to:
   a. the child's characteristics, i.e., age, sex, cognitive development
   b. type of product
   c. program content and time of airing
   d. type, position, and length of commercial
   e. the viewing context

In his second study, Ward found that:

1. Kindergarten children exhibited confusion as to what was a commercial and what was programming. Older children illustrate a more complex understanding of the commercial/program dichotomy.
2. By the second grade, about two-thirds of the sample demonstrated understanding of the commercial's role. Children's comments included: "Commercials try to get you to buy things"; "they pay for the show."
3. In general, the youngest subject had trouble separating the commercial and its role from programming. This confusion decreased rapidly with age.
4. Kindergarten children spontaneously remember food commercials, second graders toy ads.
5. Older children's recollection of commercials is more complex and coherent.
6. Younger children appear to "like" a commercial when they like the product advertised. Older children's like or dislike of commercials is more independent of their attitude toward the product. They like humorous commercials. Regardless of age, however, all children reacted favorably to entertaining ads and unfavorably to commercials they described as "dull" or "boring."
7. "Do commercials always tell the truth?" Twenty-one of 34 children 5 to 8 years of age said "yes" or "sometimes." This is contrast to the response of the 9 to 12 year old group.
Twenty-three of the 33 questioned said "no."[8]

Ward summarizes the research concerning the effect of TV advertising on 5 to 12 year old children:

> Taken as a whole, our data from pre-teenage children indicate that television advertising does indeed have an impact on children, and that impact is mediated by children's cognitive orientations, their selective attention to commercials, and in-family factors. Together with schools, peer groups and the family, television and television advertising in particular, are among the

[8]Ward, pp. 12-13.

most important inputs to gradual processes by which children acquire skills, attitudes and knowledge about the social environment.[9]

In his summary, Dr. Ward raises other important questions, including: "...what are more long-term effects of commercials on children's values?"[10]

As part of research underway at the University of Pennsylvania Wharton School of Finance and Commerce, Thomas Robertson synthesized several studies concerning TV advertising's effect on children. He concluded:

> The research data base to assess advertising's impact on the consumption behavior of children is limited and our conclusions must be quite tenuous at this point. Advertising does not have a stimulus-response effect on children, but it may have highly persuasive effects when the child is unsophisticated or relies on television for his view of reality. Advertising's potential ability to persuade may be especially high among young children who lack cognitive defenses and among ghetto children who are deprived of a balanced socialization experience. Advertising may also be instrumental in processes of attitude and preference formation among young children.[11]

What Are the Effects of TV Advertising on Adolescents?

At this point you have undoubtedly begun to form some tentative judgments concerning the effects of children's TV advertising. Whatever your views, one fact is clear. As children grow older they change. This change not only affects their own behavior but child/parent interaction. It is important then to study older children as well as the preteen-age group. There are several reasons why adolescents are an important sub-set of the advertising and children controversy.

1. They may have more credibility as purchase influencers.
2. The interaction of child and TV continues as children age.
3. The total range of adolescent behavior broadens rapidly. The effects of TV advertising may have a wider range on which to play.
4. The youth of today are important consumers in their own right.
5. Adolescence is one step closer to adulthood, where inherent attitudes and values may play a major role in consumer behavior attitudes toward advertising and business in general.
6. In many states the eighteenth birthday is now the passport for "instant adulthood" that includes drinking, gambling, voting, and marriage.

The Federal Trade Commission is concerned about the effects of TV

---

[9]Ward, p. 18.

[10]Ward, p. 19.

[11]Thomas S. Robertson, "The Impact of Television Advertising on Children," Special Issue — Marketing, *Wharton Quarterly* (Fall, 1972), p. 41.

advertising on adolescents. Dr. Daniel Wackman conducted three studies in this area and reported his findings to the F.T.C.[12]

Findings (based on samples of adolescents 12 to 19 years old):

1. Aided recall of specific advertising was very high on the average. Recall is a function of intelligence. Bright subjects with good memories scored highest on recall testing.

2. Negative attitudes toward advertising prevailed. For example, 67% of the students agreed with the statement, "Most commercials are in poor taste and are very annoying."

3. Students seemed to be neither highly materialistic nor highly non-materialistic in their value orientation.

4. Over 50% stated they had purchased one product because of TV advertising.

Buying behavior, however, is influenced most by the *frequency* (emphasis mine) of family discussions concerning consumption.[13]

In summarizing his findings Wackman states:

> The data show that TV commercials can and do cause teenagers to buy products. We do not know how much teenagers buy because of advertising, but I do not think it is likely to be very much for several reasons.[14]

These reasons include lack of programming and commercials specifically directed to adolescents, lack of useful information in advertising to adolescents, and the negative adolescent attitude toward advertising.[15] The report ends on two main themes:

1. Much more research is needed particularly into the question of why certain relationships exist.

2. Policy makers can oversimplify research data or take a policy position based on research of only one variable when several other variables have not yet been studied. Often the same data can be used to support opposing views.

Should TV Advertising to Children Be Banned? Yes!

Boston-based "Action for Children's Television" has led the fight to ban TV commercials from children's programming. In 1970 ACT petitioned the Federal Communications Commission with three proposals.

1. Elimination of all commercials from children's television.

2. Children's show hosts, performers, and cartoon characters should not be used in commercials aired on other programs.

---

[12]Daniel B. Wackman, "Effects of Television Advertising on Adolescents," Marketing Science Institute Special Report, Cambridge, Mass., 1971.

[13]Wackman, pp. 4-9.

[14]Wackman, p. 8.   [15]Wackman, p. 8.

3. To eliminate the race for mass child audience appeal each television station should provide at least 14 hours of programming per week specifically designed for children.

What caused ACT to file a petition described by the broadcasting and advertising industry as radical, unrealistic, and a bit "kooky"? There are several interrelated arguments made to support the contention that children's TV advertising should be banned.

1. Children are defenseless. Young children do not discriminate between program and commercial. They identify with commercial characters who, in turn, exercise unfair influence in generating child viewer requests for specific products.

2. Wants are created. A child can be induced to want something. Children know what they want, not what is good for them. TV may make them want candy, an expensive toy, chewable vitamins, or to be able to fly like the commercial's trade character. The primary purpose of the medium is to entertain and educate, not serve as a commercial pitchman to children.

3. Family tension results. Children bombarded by about 15 minutes of commercials per nonprime TV hour and 10 minutes per prime time hour often engage in attempts to persuade parents. Such requests and the resulting parent/child conflicts would not exist in their present intensity if TV advertising were banned.

4. Children's TV commercials are deceptive. Fast action shots of toys in use, exaggerated reactions of peers, trick camera angles that portray the product as bigger than life, pressed paper parts that appear to be metal when flashed over the screen, the "availability" of expensive optional accessories without which the toy would be meaningless, implications of strength, vigor, and athletic prowess if certain products are used, the reliance on emotional and psychological content rather than the communication of useful information — these allegations, and many more, have been made against advertisers.

5. The cumulative effect of children's advertising may have direct and harmful effects.

a. Advertising unsafe toys such as pellet shooting rifles, racers with sharp edges, dolls with removable buttons, etc., can result in direct harm to the child.

6. Poor nutritional habits may be developed early by child TV viewers.

Witnesses for Action for Children's Television testified that a child watching Channel 7, Boston, from 7:00 A.M. to 2:00 P.M. Saturday, October 28, 1972, would have seen 67 commercial messages urging him to eat or drink sweetly flavored products. ACT announced it was filing complaints with FTC against eight cereal, snack food and candy commercials monitored that Saturday.

The ads were by General Foods, Hershey Foods and Quaker Oats, for Sir Grapefellow cereal, Baron Von Redberry cereal, Pop-Tarts snack, Danish-Go-Rounds snack, Baby Ruth candy bar, Fruity Pebbles cereal, Cocoa Pebbles cereal, Froot Loops cereal, Hershey's Instant milk additive and Vanilly Crunch cereal.[16]

Robert Choate is one of the severest critics of advertising marketing food products to children.

The way to a man's heart trouble is through his stomach," reads an advertising poster in the nation's capital. The picture on the poster shows a platter of French fries, ice cream, cupcakes, pizza, spaghetti and fatty gravy. At the same time, District of Columbia children watching television on weekends are advised ten times per hour to eat French fries and ice cream (courtesy of McDonalds's), pastry (courtesy of General Foods), cupcakes (courtesy of Continental Baking), spaghetti (by Chef Boyardee) and pizza (from Shakey's and Geno's).

The heart trouble warning is all too real, but probably too late. The United States now stands eleventh among the nations of the world in adult life expectancy, and may be dropping lower. "You are what you eat" goes the slogan, and today many Americans are fat, sagging and tired. Roughly 25% of the population can be considered overweight. Even children in the elementary school playgrounds show signs of obesity. Food habits implanted from the age of 3 have visible effects by the time the child is 13 and may be earnestly regretted when he is 40.

A look at television commercials aimed at children reveals more than an advocacy of inferior foods. Twenty advertisements per hour interrupt children's programs; on prime-time adult programs, one seldom finds more than ten or twelve ads per hour. Half of the children's twenty ads sell edible products; nine out of ten of the edibles are promoted on the basis of their sugared, sweetened or "crisped" (read fried) qualities. With no accompanying warnings a child is invited ten times per hour to establish food habits which his dentist or doctor will later deplore. (Interspersed with these ads are pitches for vitamin pills sold to children in case you don't eat right.) Ten times per hour adds up to 5,000 advertisements for edibles per year, even for a moderate TV watching child. It's a course in gluttony.[17]

7. Undue stress is placed on materialistic values. Advertising stresses consumption, i.e., buying and having things as the direct route to happiness. The inverse is therefore implied — if you haven't purchased anything lately or if you don't purchase the thing advertised then you are certainly unhappy. At the 1970 White House Conference on Children the value argument was neatly and simply summarized: "Panel Chairman Fred Rogers, producer of one of television's leading children's programs, Mister

---

[16]"Kellogg, General Mills will testify before Senate Committee," *Advertising Age*, March 12, 1973, p. 75.

[17]Robert B. Choate, "The Sugar-Coated Children's Hour," *The Nation*, January 31, 1972, p. 146.

Rogers' Neighborhood, says: 'Commercials stress that in order to play you need a toy, that your mental resources are not enough.' "[18]

Should TV Advertising to Children Be Banned? No!

Arguments for the continuation of children's TV advertising are made by manufacturers of children's products, their advertising agencies, and television networks. The basic position of these advocates can be summarized into four general propositions:

1. Children's TV is in a process of evolution and improvement. The early days of both adult and children's television programming and advertising were crude by today's standards.

2. A major activity of this evolutionary development has been constant upgrading of programming to include educational, cultural, documentary, and other types of shows to balance straight entertainment.

3. There has been no malicious attempt or intent to mainpulate the child viewer. As the medium has matured, practices of the past have been modified and will continue to be modified to meet changing standards and values in broadcasting. These are scores of cases in point.

   a. self-regulation — a National Advertising Review Board has been established to review TV commercials and ensure that they meet standards of honesty and accuracy.

   b. effective January 1, 1973, the National Association of Broadcasters revised their TV code to reduce by 25% the time devoted to commercials and other nonprogram material on weekend children's TV.[19] As part of the board's action, two other important steps were taken. First, children's weekend shows will be interrupted less by commercials. Commercial interruptions are limited to not more than two per thirty-minute program and not more than four within a sixty-minute program. Also accepted was the rule that show hosts and primary cartoon characters not be used to deliver commercials within or adjacent to children's programs.

   c. manufacturers of children's vitamin products have voluntarily agreed to remove vitamin advertising from children's TV. Fred Flintstone, Bugs Bunny, and Mr. Chocolate are out of the vitamin selling business. Bristol-Myers Co. (Pals Multiple Vitamins), Hoffman-LaRoche, Inc. (Zestabs), and Miles Laboratories, Inc. (Chocks, Bugs Bunny, and Flintstone Chewable Vitamins) withdrew an estimated $4 million worth of children's TV advertising budgets as of June 1, 1972.[20]

[18] "Advertising — Quieting the Children's Hour," *Time,* April 19, 1971, p. 75.

[19] "N.A.B. TV Board Votes a 25% Cut in Ads for Children," *New York Times,* January 22, 1972, p. 59.

[20] "Bugs Bunny Quitting Vitamin Sales Game During Kids TV Time," *The Wall Street Journal,* July 21, 1972, p. 15.

d. in spite of the fact that early research indicates below par preference for educational fare TV, networks are upgrading programming simultaneously with correcting advertising abuses. NBC substituted "Take a Giant Step" for cartoon programming. The new show is designed to "stimulate children to make decisions, assume responsibility, and understand their goals and aspirations."[21] ABC's quality entry, "Curiosity Shop," combines the elements of "entertainment, education, and stimulation."[22] (It is interesting to note that the regular CBS show, Sabrina the Teenage Witch, got higher ratings than the two "quality" shows combined.)

4. Considering the preceding factors, children's TV practices need to be continually studied and improved. This can best be achieved as advertisers, the broadcasting industry, appropriate government regulatory agencies, and consumer groups work together to achieve meaningful children's programming with a sound economic base.

What Would Happen If Children's TV Advertising Were Banned?

The presence of the TV advertiser is not without benefits to the child audience, to parents, and to society as a whole.

1. Advertising pays the bill. Advertisers pay for the privilege of using the airwaves. It is their payment for commercial time that makes it possible for the networks to air special programming for children. While public broadcasting provides a meaningful supplement to sponsored TV, its viewers represent only a small part of the total TV audience. Reacting to the ACT proposal for commercial-less children's TV and the 14 hours per week of children's programming concept, Television Information Office executive Roy Danish offered this analysis:

> ...the production of 14 hours a week of children's programs at a cost equivalent to that of *Sesame Street* would place network expenditures in the range of $130 million to $140 million a year. He pointed out that the networks in the 1970s made a total profit of about $50 million in 1970 and said an outlay of $130-$140 million without sponsorship would leave the companies with a deficit of about $75 million.[23]

2. Advertising helps in socializing and in initiating the child for a lifelong consumer role. In a market economy, people are faced with insatiable desires and limited resources. Learning to discriminate between consumption alternatives and fairly presented advertising helps prepare the

[21]"Kid's TV: Assessing the New 'Quality'," *The Wall Street Journal*, September 23, 1971, p. 18.

[22]"Kid's TV," p. 18.

[23]"Debating Advertising and Children's TV," *Broadcasting Magazine*, October 25, 1971, p. 43.

child for adolescence and adulthood where personal resources, economic motivation, and consumer wants must be balanced.

3. The TV advertiser has a right, the parent a responsibility. Parents present an interesting variable in the children's TV controversy. They want the freedom that the TV-occupied child does not restrict, they want expensive original programming, they want educational betterment for their children — all understandable objectives. On the other hand, some parents and critical parent groups wish to totally eliminate the economic incentive for the sponsor but still rely on TV as a surfeit baby-sitter.

> ... rather than blame the TV advertiser for making his product as appealing as possible, parents should exercise their responsibility by letting their children know that the world is not entirely their oyster, that they can't have every doll that burps, cries, gurgles and coos its way into their hearts.
>
> Both advertisers and broadcasters have very real obligations of their own when it comes to TV advertising and programming, of course. And there are indications that they are beginning to live up to these obligations in the form of more educational programs and less intensive and high-powered commercials.
>
> But the final — and initial arbiter of children's tastes and morality is the parent. This is one responsibility they can't shun — or shunt on to others.[24]

4. Don't throw out the baby with the bath water. The critics of children's TV advertising and programming have recommended extreme "solutions" to the "problem." Arguments are impassioned, emotional, and, for the most part, sincere. Television advertisers and the broadcasting industry are portrayed as sinister villains who cleverly manipulate and poison the values of children. And yet, not even the most objective and skillful researcher can explain the effects of children's TV advertising. Research results are very carefully qualified and the limitations of current evidence stressed. Policymakers are warned that results are tentative, incomplete, and based on small numeric and geographic samples. No longitudinal research has yet been completed. The data suggest that advertising is only one of many variables affecting the child consumer. Further, children soon become skeptical viewers and filter out commercial messages, rejecting many, being entertained by some, and being influenced by a few. The limited research currently available does not support the drastic recommendations proposed. In our emotional haste toward an immediate and "final solution" we may indeed throw out the baby with the bath water.

Postscript

Please forgive a loving father (myself) for getting his daughter Sarah and

[24] "What About Parents," *Advertising Age,* July 26, 1971, p. 16.

his son Richard into the act. Two events of interest occurred during the writing of this chapter that are directly related to TV advertising and children and to the broader topic, marketing and children.

Research evidence suggests that young children (pre-kindergarten) do not clearly differentiate between program content and commercials. One afternoon Sarah and Rich were watching "Flipper." Dinnertime arrived and the children, watching TV in the den, were called, asked to turn the TV off, and to come to the table. They did not respond. I went in and noted four bright little eyes glued to a "Charlie the Tuna" commercial for Starkist brand tuna. Thinking about the commercial was of no interest to the kids, I flicked the set off and started to leave the room. Sarah, then two and a half, screamed and started to cry. When I finally got her quieted, I asked, "What's the matter?"

She replied, "But Dad, I *like* that *show!*" Congratulations Charlie!

A large envelope was delivered, addressed to my son, Richard W. Wheatley, Among the many materials inside the envelope was a card with the following inscription:

Official Member
SALES LEADERSHIP CLUB
this is to certify that

Name ....

Address ....

has been enrolled in the Sales Leadership Club as an Official Member. As such, he is entitled to all the privileges of membership and is fully authorized to sell SLC products and earn guaranteed SLC prizes.

SALES LEADERSHIP CLUB
Springfield, Massachusetts

The remaining contents included a four-page miniature "newspaper" containing photos and testimonials from 38 children or their parents thanking SLC for the opportunity to sell their quality products, discussing the benefits of being in business, and/or describing the prizes won. A two-page cover letter detailing the proposition and aimed at persuading the young entrepreneur to sign up was included. Quite a package for a three and a half year old!

Discussion Questions

1. Relate the concept of causality to the assertion that advertising makes children buy.
2. a. List and discuss several factors in addition to TV advertising that influence ultimate purchase decisions.
   b. Attempt to rank these influential variables is descending order of their importance for a specific consumer, product, and environment.
3. Identify and contrast the variables that influenced your decision to purchase:
   a. The brand and model of car you now drive or plan to purchase.
   b. The brand of soft drink or beer you prefer.
4. Discuss the contrasting points of view presented in the following quotations:
   a. "Business is to be condemned because advertising creates unnecessary wants and needs, manipulating the individual to do that which he normally would not."
   b. "Needs are innate. They cannot be created. Advertising brings to the market alternative ways in which consumers may satisfy their needs and desires."
   c. "Man is a combination of economic and emotional drives. Some products are purchased to satisfy purely functional (economic) requirements, some to satisfy purely emotional requirements. Most purchases satisfy some combination of economic and emotional needs. Society seems unwilling to acknowledge that man has emotional needs and that advertising merely reflects the values and needs of the society in which it operates."
5. Is advertising good or bad?
   a. Evaluate the opposing points of view presented in the chapter and in other sources.
   b. Express and defend your own conclusion.
6. "The best thing that could happen to the auto buyer would be for Detroit to build a car that would last 25 years."
   a. How do you react? Why?
   b. What social advantages and disadvantages are associated with product obsolescence?
   c. How would advertising be changed if fashion obsolescence were eliminated? If technological obsolescence were controlled?
7. "Children's TV advertising critics' objections are valid because they are based on moral values, whereas the defenses of business are based only on economic values."
   a. Carefully evaluate this statement.
   b. Elaborate on the implications involved.
   c. Do you agree with the value rating and conclusion?
8. What are the limitations associated with research evidence presented concerning the effects of TV advertising?
9. Contrast advertising effects on young children (2-5), children (6-12), and adolescents (13-18).
10. Assume you had the power to (1) prevent any change in TV advertising to children and adolescents, (2) modify current practice, (3) totally ban TV commercials on children's programs.
    a. What would you do?
    b. Why?

11. What is your opinion concerning the relative harm done by children's program content vs. commercials?

12. In your view:
   a. What is the responsibility of the parent concerning children's TV?
   b. What is the advertiser's responsibility?
   c. What is the TV station manager's or network's responsibility?

13. Assume TV commercials were banned from children's (age 2-12) programs.
   a. Who should pay for production and showing costs?
   b. Who should make decisions concerning program content?

14. "Part of TV's mission is to entertain, to provide comic relief, vicarious thrills. In the adult audience ancient reruns of 'I Love Lucy,' and 'Gomer Pyle' are better received than 'Masterpiece Theater.' It's not surprising that 'Sabrina' outpolls shows like 'Giant Step.' Children, as well as adults, need balanced programming. Those who would force cartoons and fun shows from the air may do more harm than good."
   a. How do you react?

15. Concerning the broader topic area of marketing to children what freedoms and restrictions would you recommend? Again consider the responsibilities of marketers, government, and parents in the formulation of your response.

16. React to this statement: "Attempts to have the government ban TV advertising to children is another example of the abdication of individual values, rights, and responsibilities. Our society continues to give up its freedom of action and alternatives on the false assumption that the government can make and enforce optimum social policy."

Suggested Class Projects

1. Hold a mock government hearing on the question "Should TV advertising to children be banned?"
   a. Organize two panels, one for and one against the ban.
   b. Review the chapter materials and outside sources.
   c. Present evidence giving equal time to both sides, as well as 10 minutes to each side for rebuttal.
   d. Have the class vote on the issue at the conclusion of the hearings.

2. a. Carefully analyze the original research summarized in the chapter.
   b. Identify areas for further research concerning advertising effects on children.
   c. Clearly define the problem(s) and develop a research design which could be implemented.

3. a. Select a recently purchased shopping good such as a car, appliance, furniture, or clothing.
   b. Working back from the purchase, attempt to identify the specific shopping behavior you engaged in prior to the purchase and the various influences which resulted in the selection of what you purchased over alternative brands, styles, etc.
   c. Prepare a schematic diagram of your search and the influence inputs during the search process.
   d. How much and in what way did advertising play a part in this process?

4. a. Develop a simple set of questions concerning children's reactions to TV advertising.

    b. Select a sample group of young children and a sample group of adolescents.
    c. Conduct a group discussion based on your questions — tape record the sessions.
    d. Analyze and report the data and related conclusions.
    Note: A wide variety of informal research projects may be conducted. Respondents may include parents, advertising agency personnel, broadcasters, businessmen, officials of regulatory agencies, etc. A large class could divide respondents, do independent research, and then synthesize and compare results by respondent group.

    5. a. Invite: (1) a representative of ACT.
            (2) a representative of a manufacturing firm currently advertising on children's TV.
      b. Have each present their views concerning children's TV advertising.
      c. Hold an open discussion in which the class participates.
      d. As an alternative you might invite each participant separately and give each sufficient time for a full presentation and discussion. After the class has heard both sides devote a subsequent period to class debate and discussion of each presentation.

    6. a. Secure a copy of the evaluative criteria for children's TV advertising used by the National Advertising Review Board.
      b. Critically review the criteria.
      c. What additions and deletions would you implement?
      d. How do you feel about "self-regulation"?

    7. a. Select a sample of children's TV shows.
      b. Develop a scorecard of values stressed in (1) programming and (2) advertising.
      c. Analyze, compare, and contrast program values and commercial content.

    8. a. Spend a Saturday morning viewing children's TV commercials.
      b. Identify commercials which you find objectionable (be certain to specify why).
      c. Identify commercials to which you do not object.
      d. Based on this experience develop a scorecard that could be used to screen children's TV commercials.

Supplementary Readings

Books

Blackman, Jules. *Advertising and Competition.* New York: New York University Press, 1967.
Boyd, Harper W., and Levy, Sidney J. *Promotion: A Behavioral View.* Englewood Cliffs, N.J.: Prentice-Hall, 1967.
Brumbaugh, Florence. "What Effect Does Advertising Have on Children?" In *Children and TV,* edited by Constance Carr, pp. 20-43. Washington, D.C.: Association for Childhood Education International, 1954.
Kollat, David T., et al., eds. *Research in Consumer Behavior.* New York: Holt, Rinehart and Winston, 1970.
Lavidge, Robert, and Holloway, Robert J., eds. *Marketing and Society.* Homewood, Ill.: Richard D. Irwin, Inc., 1969.

McNeal, James V. *Children as Consumers.* Austin Tex.: University of Texas Bureau of Business Research, 1964.
Marketing Science Institute. *Advertising Measurement and Decision Making.* Boston: Allyn & Bacon, 1968.
Martineau, Pierre. *Motivation in Advertising.* New York: McGraw-Hill, 1957.
Piaget, I. *The Child's Conception of the World.* Totowa, N.J.: Littlefield, Adams & Co., 1965.
Sargent, Hugh W., ed. *Frontiers of Advertising Theory and Research.* Palo Alto, Calif.: Pacific Books, 1972.
Wheatley, John J., ed. *Measuring Advertising Effectiveness – Selected Readings.* Homewood, Ill.: Richard D. Irwin, Inc., 1969.

Articles

"Advertisers Wary of FTC 'Proposals' for Children's Ads" *Broadcasting,* August 20, 1973, pp. 71, 72.
Arlen, Michael S. "A Few Sensible Words About Children's TV." *McCalls* February 1971, pp. 34-38.
Blake, Richard A. "Children's TV; Ethics and Economics." *America,* October 31, 1972, pp. 308-311.
"Broadcasters' TV Code Unit Eliminating One-Third of Weekend Commercial Time." *Wall Street Journal,* January 7, 1972, p. 12.
"Bugs Bunny Quitting Vitamin Sales During Kids's TV Time." *Wall Street Journal,* July 21, 1972, p. 15.
"Cereal Makers Say Nutrition Hearings Rigged; Won't Appear." *Advertising Age,* March 5, 1973. p. 1.
"Children's Ads, Self-Concept Themes Need More Regulation, Authors Say." *Advertising Age,* March 12, 1973. p. 1.
"The Children's Hour: Stunned by Criticism." *Wall Street Journal,* September 10, 1971, p. 1.
"Debating Advertising and Children's Television." *Broadcasting,* October 25, 1971, p. 43.
Federal Communications Commission Annual Report: Fiscal 1971. "Children's Programs." p. 36.
Federal Communications Commission Annual Report: Fiscal 1972. "Toy Ads," p. 36.
Frideres, James S. "Advertising, Buying Patterns and Children." *Journal of Advertising Research* 3 (1973): 34-35.
McDonald, Colin. "What is the Short-term Effect of Advertising?" Cambridge, Mass.: Marketing Science Institute, 1971.
"Quieting the Children's Hour." *Time,* April 19, 1971, p. 75.
Robertson, Thomas S. "The Impact of Television Advertising on Children." *The Wharton Quarterly* (Fall 1972): 38-41. Special issue on Marketing.
Shayon, Robert Louis. "Birth of a Salesman." *Saturday Review,* February 5, 1972, p. 5.
"The Sugar Coated Children's Hour." *The Nation,* January 31, 1972, pp. 146-148.
"Telecasters Change Kids' TV; Study Finds Moppets Cynical." *Advertising Age,* July 19, 1971, p. 1.
"Television Ads Aimed at Children Stir Ire of Parents, Critics." *Wall Street Journal,* October 22, 1970. p. 1.

"Three Vitamin Makers Leave Children's TV." *Advertising Age,* July 26, 1972, pp. 2-3.

"Toy Makers Prepare for Battle with Code Board." *Advertising Age,* October 9, 1972, p. 3.

Wackman, Daniel B. "Effects of Television Advertising on Adolescents." Cambridge, Mass.: Marketing Science Institute, 1971.

Ward, Scott. "Children and Promotion: New Consumer Battleground?" Cambridge, Mass.: Marketing Science Institute, 1972.

Ward, Scott. "Effects of Television Advertising on Children." Cambridge, Mass.: Marketing Science Institute, 1971.

Ward, Scott. "Kids' TV — Marketers on Hot Seat." *Harvard Business Review* (July-Aug. 1972): 16.

Ward, Scott, and Wackman, Daniel. "Children's Purchase Influence Attempts and Parental Yielding." *Journal of Marketing Research* (Aug. 1972): 316-319.

Ward, Scott, and Wackman, Daniel B. "Family and Media Influences on Adolescent Consumer Learning." *American Behavioral Scientist* 14 (1971): 415-427.

Ward, Scott; Reale, Craig; and Levinson, David. "Children's Perceptions, Explanations, and Judgments of Television Advertising: A Further Explanation." Cambridge, Mass.: Marketing Science Institute, 1972.

Wells, William D. "Communicating With Children." *Journal of Advertising Research* 5 (1973): 34-35.

"What About Parents?" *Advertising Age,* July 26, 1971, p. 16.

4

Energy Versus Ecology—
The Santa Barbara Blowout

The curve in the breathtaking coast of Southern California, beginning at Ventura and climaxing at Point Conception, cradles the Santa Barbara Channel. The Channel is bordered on the Pacific side by four islands, Anacapa, Santa Cruz, Santa Rosa, and San Miguel, stretching some sixty miles from east to west. What a view! From the city of Santa Barbara and its palm lined beaches, tourists and natives alike enjoyed one of nature's perfect vistas. Well, almost perfect. Twelve oil drilling platforms jutted from the channel's ocean floor.

Depending on your sensitivity, you ignored, became accustomed to, or harbored deep resentment toward these unnatural alterations to an otherwise perfect seascape. Eight platforms were located inside the state of California's three-mile limit. The remaining four platforms were riveted to the Channel floor between the state's three-mile limit and the federal offshore twelve-mile limit. This close proximity was not a very comforting thought to those who had opposed the drilling. Why had the oil industry come to the Santa Barbara Channel? To find oil, of course. Oil that an insatiable nation consumed with abandon. Oil that might be within easy reach and close to refining and marketing centers. Specifically, who was interested in platforms A and B located in federal waters, slightly east of the Santa Barbara waterfront?

The people of the United States were interested. Your government had received $61,418,000 in cash, plus 16⅔% royalty per barrel, plus a modest annual lease rental fee of $16,200. These payments were received in exchange for drilling rights on 5,400 acres of land under the Santa Barbara Channel. The consortium leasing the development rights included Union Oil, Gulf Oil, Mobil Oil, and Texaco.[1]

Because of the adjacency to the Santa Barbara coast, Union Oil's platforms A and B were a particular sore spot with city and area residents. Journalist Robert Easton provides the following sketch of the man-made structure and soon-to-be villain, Platform A.

[1] For one of the best full accounts of the Santa Barbara oil spill, see Robert Easton, *Black Tide* (New York: Delacorte Press, 1972).

The platform stood in 188 feet of water. The top of its vertical drilling rig reached 210 feet above the surface of the sea. Its structural framework of steel pipes weighed about 3,000 tons. Steel pilings inside its hollow legs had been driven into the ocean floor to stabilize it against wind, wave, and earthquake. Its superstructure supported two 115 by 134-foot decks, drilling slots for 56 wells, a galley and lounge, sleeping quarters for a dozen men, workshops, and a helipad. There was, in addition, a slant-drilling rig, protruding at an angle of about 30 degrees, for tapping oil sands that lay too near the ocean floor to be tapped by the vertical rig. A 34,000 volt submarine cable brought power to the platform from shore, and a submarine pipeline was ready to carry its petroleum to onshore processing plants. Platform A had cost about $5 million. Each of its 56 wells would cost about a quarter million more.[2]

The Event

The following account summarizes the oil spill, beginning with the "blowout" of oil well A-21 and ending when water borne crude oil reached the harbors and beaches of Santa Barbara.[3]

Prologue:

Prior to January 28, 1969, four oil wells had been drilled from Platform A. These wells were waiting to be put into production. The wells were in the same general area as well A-21 and had been drilled through similar ground formations with no ill effects.

January 28, 1969; 10:45 A.M.:

The oil crew employed by Peter Bowden Drilling, Inc., the drilling contractor for Union Oil, had drilled A-21 to its maximum depth of 3,479 feet. The crew was moving 90-foot sections of drill pipe from the hole. As the eighth section of pipe was being disconnected at the deck level, a loud, hissing sound suddenly filled the air. The top of pipe section eight, 90 feet above the deck level, suddenly spewed a mixture of gas and drilling mud on the deck, equipment, and men below. As the crew disconnected the pipe at deck level, the gas and mud erupted at their feet, propelling a roaring spume 20 feet above the deck. "Well, A-21 had blown out, and the largest disaster of its kind in U.S. history had begun."[4]

The blowout is "sealed":

Three valiant efforts were made by the crew to seal off the volcano now erupting at their feet. First an attempt was made to screw a 75-pound emergency check valve into the pipe's mouth. This immediately proved a futile gesture. Next the crew attempted to position a 30-foot section of pipe so that it could be forced into the erupting casing. This pipe could be connected to the mud pumps and mud forced into the casing to seal the

[2]Easton, p. 7.   [3]Easton, pp. 6-46.
[4]Easton, p. 8.

blowout. In the increasingly difficult and dangerous working conditions, however, the equipment fouled and was rendered inoperative. It was clear that the final emergency measure would have to be taken. Approximately 13 minutes after the eighth section of pipe had been disconnected on Platform A, the remaining 2,759 feet of drill pipe was dropped to the bottom of the hole. The crew activated the "blind rams." These 20-inch wide by 4-inch thick plates were surfaced with tight, sealing bonded rubber. The rams were activated by a huge 4-ton valve. The drill pipe dropped and the massive rams came together from opposite directions, crimping and sealing the erupting pipe like a giant pair of pliers.

The Channel Floor Rupture

It is not clear precisely when the first bubbles and boils caused by escaping gas were sighted. But certainly within 30 minutes after A-21 had gone wild, boils began to appear in the vicinity of Platform A and Platform B, about one-half mile distant. The ocean floor had ruptured. By 1:00 P.M. Union Oil's offshore production superintendent had reported the blowout to the appropriate agency of the Interior Department and to the Coast Guard. The Union Oil official reported that there was no oil mixed with the surfacing gas but asked that the Coast Guard stand by. Meanwhile, Union would proceed with operations in an attempt to regain control of the well.

The Communication Gap

Union Oil did not contact the Coast Guard again that day. Late that afternoon (January 28), however, County Supervisor Daniel Grant was meeting with Governor Reagan and other government officials in the county administration building. The group had just toured areas near Carpenteria, which had been damaged by floods. During the meeting, Grant was handed a note asking him to take an urgent phone call. Grant requested that the call be placed later or a message left since he was in an important meeting with the governor. No message was left, nor did Grant receive a subsequent call at home that evening. Union Oil had attempted to inform Santa Barbara officials concerning the A-21 blowout, but, in the jargon of communications theory, when there was a sender, there was no receiver, and when there was a receiver, there was no sender.

First Word of Oil

At approximately 5:45 P.M. the Coast Guard officer notified earlier by Union concerning the blowout received a phone call at home. The caller was from the State Department of Fish and Game. During the conversation, the caller stated that Union Oil had called his department's Los Angeles office less than an hour before. Union reported that a well in tract 402 had blown out and was losing oil. Within the hour, Mr. Craggs of Union confirmed that he (Craggs) had just returned from the area and that oil as well as gas was rising to the Channel surface. Throughout the night, the Union crew worked in vain to stop the oil.

The Morning After

About 8:00 A.M., January 29, 1969, a Coast Guard officer and a State Fish and Game warden got their first in-person view of the developing tragedy from a Coast Guard helicopter. "It looked like a world gone wrong. The slick's heaviest concentration, brownish black, reached southward — or seaward — from the platform for a distance of half a mile. There it thinned and continued southerly for about four miles. Then it veered southeast toward the shore for another mile. A rainbow-colored area extended for two miles west and two to four miles east of the main slick. A similar rainbowed area extended eight to ten miles south of the platform."[5]

The Word is Out

Soon after the Coast Guard helicopter arrived over the Channel, public officials, Union Oil executives, and news media representatives were gathering to discuss the worsening situation. By that evening the public was to learn what was still known by relatively few. The oil and gas gushing through fissures and porous sand on the bottom of Santa Barbara Channel were now out of control. The human reactions to the continuing spill and the prospect of the oil reaching land were quick and initially emotional. Two county officials, chairmen of the Channel Oil Advisory Committee and the County Planning Director, fired a telegram off to the newly inaugurated President Richard Nixon:

> Major oil spill verified in Santa Barbara Channel from drilling operation on platform in federal waters. Department of Interior and oil industry said prior to leaving that safeguards would prevent such major spillage. Since they are not adequate, request immediate cessation of all oil drilling in federal waters in Santa Barbara Channel, pending investigation and permanent correction. Request is not limited to platform in question, but to all such platforms.[6]

The Coast Guard was accused of acting too slowly in reporting the blowout to responsible county officials. Oil in general and Union Oil in particular were held to be the major villains. Information concerning the specifics of the blowout and the growing slick appeared to vary by source. Union's most recent estimate of the slick's size was approximately five square miles. A Coast Guard official estimated the slick's size at 100 square miles. During the next few days, the rate of oil flow from the Channel floor was initially estimated at:

a. 21,000 gallons per day by Union Oil;

[5]Easton, p. 19.   [6]Easton, pp. 20-21.

b. 210,000 gallons per day by a scientist associated with a private research firm;

c. 170,000 gallons per day by a Department of Interior official.

Under conditions of stress, emotion, and a lack of precise information, an atmosphere of suspicion developed. Was Union Oil being candid? Did federal interests identify more with their leasing tenants or with residents of Santa Barbara? Had the Coast Guard acted promptly? Were the area residents realistic and rational concerning oil in general?

A Plan of Action

At 9:00 P.M. that evening, public and private officials met. A loose network of plans and the organizational structure for their implementation had been developed under former President Lyndon Johnson. This national plan was a result of the *Torrey Canyon* oil spill in 1967. When this grounded tanker's hull split open, an estimated thirty-million gallons of crude oil spilled into the adjacent waters off Seven Stones Reef, England. In addition to the National Multiagency Oil and Hazardous Materials Contingency Plan, the *Torrey Canyon* incident spurred development of the Coast Guard's Marine Chemical Disaster Plan. During the meeting, the Coast Guard plan was to be the catalyst which mobilized the lines of defense against the ever-widening slick. The district Coast Guard commander, a young lieutenant, assumed responsibility for coordinating the defense. Union Oil agreed to assume responsibility for stopping the oil flow, for protection of the harbor, and for cleaning up whatever damage the slick might cause. Shortly before the meeting was adjourned, Platform A was evacuated due to imminent danger of explosion and fire caused by escaping gas.

Oil Reaches Shore

The observation of the newly formed slick made on January 29, 1969, indicated that the oil was drifting away from the mainland. On January 30 however, the wind and current were slowly pushing oil toward shore. The total slick area was now estimated at 150 square miles. In addition to the mainland, a small and separate slick was drifting toward the Channel Islands. Union Oil was busy erecting barriers at strategic harbor locations. The slick was being bombed by thousands of gallons of chemicals. These chemicals were designed to break the slick into minute droplets that could be easily consumed by bacteria. In a controversy surrounded by controversy, the use of these chemicals was to become a major issue. Work had also resumed on platform A.

That afternoon, oil had made its way through the kelp beds and surf at Rincon. The next day, the slick covered about 200 square miles. Before the first week of February was over, several land areas as well as Santa

Barbara's harbor and beaches had been oiled. Oil, which ranked a close second to the dog as man's best friend, was suddenly man's greatest enemy. In addition to man, oil was now making life difficult for bird, animal, and fish life in the Santa Barbara ecosystem. While it was too early to know the full effect, hundreds of sea birds were dead and dying and the coast's precious marine mammals — sea lions, seals, and whales — appeared to be in mortal danger. What oil would do to the undersea life remained a troublesome unknown.

The Remaining Events

There is no pretense in the previous sections or in this summary of presenting every important detail concerning the Santa Barbara oil spill. While the remainder of the chapter is dedicated to giving equal time to those involved in the ensuing controversy, you will have to examine and evaluate additional detailed evidence before arriving at your personal conclusions concerning the incident. The summary of events following oil's landfall at Santa Barbara is presented in an effort to provide focus on key subsequent developments and as a framework for further analysis.[7]

1969

January 31 GOO (Get Oil Out) founded. This private group would become a large and powerful adversary of oil interests.

February 1 The slick covers 200 square miles, but favorable winds keep most of it at sea. Sierra Club wires Interior Secretary Hickel protesting use of chemicals.

February 3 Slick now 350 square miles. Interior Secretary personally inspects area and asks oil firms to voluntarily stop drilling. The oil firms comply.

February 4 Anacapa Island, a home colony for seals, innundated by oil. Slick now 500 square miles. Government permits some firms to resume drilling.

February 5 Oil on Santa Barbara beaches. The booms have failed to keep oil out of the harbor. Black crude oil six inches deep sloshes against Santa Barbara's fleet of pleasure boats. Man appears relatively helpless as oil continues gushing from the Channel floor and the slick is estimated at 800 square miles.

February 7 All Channel oil operations, except the frantic attempts to seal A-21, are ordered stopped by Hickel. By midnight A-21 is plugged by cement. Premature clean-up efforts feature straw. Straw absorbs oil and is used heavily on the beaches. Chemicals still in dispute and waves wash oil over barrier booms.

[7]This chronology is adapted from Jinnie Huglin, "Diary of a Disaster," *McCalls,* June 1970, p. 58.

February 8 Oil's effect on sea birds becomes painfully visible. "We know from the papers that most of the birds are doomed, but we do what we can. We lift them from pools of thick crude oil or from the tangles of straw and kelp. Once captured, after the first panic, they sit quietly enough in their cardboard boxes.

"All of them seem to go through a pathetic stylized dance of death. At first, flapping their winds in the black water, hoping that this will shake off the unknown enemy. Then, tragically, they preen themselves with their beaks. At last, weakened by struggling against waves and oil, they wash ashore. Then comes the tragic-comic race to catch them. If they have enough strength left, they return to the water, the water that has always been their refuge but is now their destruction. Our sad waiting goes on. Finally, exhausted, the bedraggled birds drift in and slowly push themselves out of the water. When I wrap a towel or piece of an old sheet around their bodies, they stab at my hands in fear."[8]

February 9 Governor Reagan declares Santa Barbara a disaster area.

February 13 Various clean-up measures continue as oil again overflows from Channel rupture.

February 17 Oil firms ordered by Hickel to pay damage and clean-up costs. Oil ordered pumped from Platform A in an attempt to relieve underground pressure.

February 23 New leak near platform A. Five wells now producing in an effort to relieve pressure. Oil flow and contamination of Santa Barbara appears to be increasing.

February 28 Leak flowing heavily again.

March 5 Leak slacking now. Apparently the worst is over. Clean-up efforts continue. Twenty-seven wells now in production.

April 3 Secretary Hickel authorizes resumption of drilling on five federally owned leases in Santa Barbara Channel.

April 5 The city and county of Santa Barbara bring legal action against Secretary Hickel and oil firms as drilling activities resume.

June 2 A bombshell! Nixon's scientific advisors recommend *more* drilling — up to fifty wells. "To relieve oil pressure" is the reason given. "It may take ten to twenty years for this."[9]

Get Oil Out? Yes!

Within hours after the news of the A-21 blowout was made public, private citizens in Santa Barbara began to mobilize a massive effort to get oil out of the Santa Barbara Channel. "GOO" was headed by Alvin C. Weingand, a former California state legislator. GOO became the catalyst

[8]Huglin, p. 64.   [9]Huglin, p. 130.

for public indignation. Eventually over 100,000 people signed the GOO petition to President Nixon, demanding cessation of oil prospecting and producing in the Channel. Why should oil be forced to leave? Several of the key arguments are summarized in the following paragraphs.

Geological conditions

Drilling operations should have never been permitted in the first place. The Channel floor is unstable. Furthermore, Southern California is prime earthquake country.

> ... the area in which the drilling took place was known from the outset to be extremely hazardous. That is, drilling was occurring on an ocean bottom known for its extraordinary geological circumstances — porous sand lacking a bedrock "ceiling" capable of restraining uncontrollably seeping oil. Thus, the continuing leakage through the sands at various points above the oil reservoir cannot be stopped, and this could have been predicted from the data known to all parties involved.
>
> Another peculiarity of the Channel that had been known to the experts is the fact that it is located in the heart of earthquake activity in a region that is among the most earthquake prone in the country. Santa Barbarans are now asking what might occur during an earthquake; if pipes on the ocean floor and casings through the ocean bottom should be sheared, the damage done by the Channel's thousands of potential producing wells would devastate the entire coast of Southern California.[10]

Territorial Rights

Who owns offshore waters and related submerged lands? This question had plagued coastal states, the federal government, and various international agencies for centuries. Today state jurisdiction ends at the three-mile limit. Under law, the federal government has jurisdiction outside this slim coastline border. This is hardly fair. The resources of a coastal state should be controlled by that state. In cases where citizens wish to forego economic gain to protect the environment, they should have the opportunity to do so.

> For over fifteen years, Santa Barbara's political leaders attempted to prevent the despoliation of their coastline by oil drilling in adjacent federal waters. Although they were unsuccessful in blocking the leasing of *federal* waters beyond the three-mile limit, they were able to establish a sanctuary within *state* waters (thus foregoing the adjacent localities). It was therefore a great irony that the one city which had voluntarily exchanged revenue for a pure environment should find itself faced, in January of 1969, with a massive eruption which was ultimately to cover the entire city coastline with a thick coat of crude oil. The air was soured for many hundreds of feet inland, and tourism — the traditional economic base of the region — was severely threatened. After ten days, the runaway well was brought under control, only to erupt again in February. This fissure was closed in March, but was followed by a sustained "seepage" of oil — a leakage which continues today

[10]Harvey Molotch, "Oil in the Velvet Playground," *Ramparts*, November 1969, pp. 47-48.

to pollute the sea, the air and the famed local beaches. The oil companies had paid a record $603 million for their lease rights, and neither they nor the federal government bore any significant legal responsibility toward the localities which those lease rights might endanger.[11]

Technological Lag

We have a proven technological skill for methodically destroying our environment but little talent and interest in applying technology to its improvement. As a minimum precaution, no further drilling should be permitted until means can be developed to quickly and thoroughly clean up the inevitable oil spills that will result. The Santa Barbara incident demonstrated how feeble and helpless man becomes when his technology goes awry. The following summary of clean-up "technology" proves how helpless we really are.

Clean Up Methods — A Tragic Comedy

a. Chemical bombing. Chemical dispersements may break up slick but also have a toxic effect on living things.

b. Barrier booms. Long floating booms with hanging plastic skirts are supposed to contain the slick. Wind and wave action washes oil over the booms, so they are of little value.

c. Vacuum cleaner. A High rigid steel "V" is dragged through the slick to herd the oil toward a siphon tube that sucks up the oil and pumps it to a barge. Weather is again a key variable.

d. A lid on the leak. A steel cap is placed over the leak. Shaped like an inverted funnel, it is supposed to channel the oil for siphoning. A total failure.

e. The bubble machine. Air is forced through perforated pipe. Rising surface bubbles provide some resistance to the slick's movement.

f. Cement clouds. Powdery cement sprayed on oil to coagulate droplets. Surface winds whisk powder away from target.

g. Blankets. Two blankets of nylon cloth and plastic cover the leaks. No noticeable effect.

h. Burning. Oil on water can be ignited, resulting in air pollution. The residue on the surface after burning must still be cleaned up.

i. Sinking. A sinking solution was used to take about 20,000 tons to the bottom of the Bay of Biscay. However, the danger to sea life is as yet unknown.

j. The last straw. Absorbent straw is still the most effective clean-up tool. Straw is spread over the oil and given time to become saturated and then is collected and carried off for disposal. How sophisticated can you get!

[11]Molotch, p. 44.

Life Systems Damage

As each species is destroyed, we move one step closer to the extinction of man himself. Approximately 3,500 to 4,000 seabirds were killed by the oil slick and its effects. The *Torrey Canyon* disaster is estimated to have killed 25,000 birds. The survival rate of treated Santa Barbara birds was about 10%. The long-term effects on whales, sea lions, seals, porpoises, fishes, and other indigenous fauna cannot yet be fully assessed. Of greater potential danger than the immediate loss of life or the ability to reproduce of any one species is the potential disruption in the aquatic food chain. The food chain is based on microscopic plankton that serve as the staple for larger species which, in turn, provide food for larger species, etc. To interrupt the food chain progression at any level is to endanger the entire ecosystem. Man is at the end of the chain as he consumes the products of the sea. In addition, some toxins may be stored in the flesh of shellfish and other seafood. These toxins are then ingested by man.

What was the effect of the spill?

> First, we do not know all the answers — We will probably never know all the answers. This is due partly to the complex interaction of forces operating in the area at the time of the spill and partly to general lack of knowledge of the ecology of the area. True, some background data were available, but not enough to answer the question in full.
>
> Several factors that complicated the problem of determining the effects of the oil spill were operative in the Santa Barbara Channel at the time of the spill. There were active natural oil seeps in the area. Was the oil on the beaches all from the spill, or was part of it from natural seepage? How did the natural seepage influence the ecology of the Santa Barbara Channel? The spill occurred during a period of unusually heavy rains, with peak flooding on January 25 and February 25. In some areas, the biota was under stress at the time of the spill from lowered salinities, increased sedimentation, and possibly an increase in pesticides. Here the task was to differentiate between effects covered by these environmental factors, the oil spill and possible synergistic effects.[12]

Jacques Cousteau made the following statement in a 1970 interview relative to sinking: "Imagine how clever of mankind, when he has a big slick of poison on top of the water, to add something to it that will make it sink slowly and kill everything in its path, all the way to the bottom."[13]

The Economic Effects

We are told we must have oil. The economics involved dictate that we seek and take oil wherever we can. You seldom hear about the negative economic effects of an oil accident on the area involved.

[12]Dale Straughan, "What Has Been the Effect of the Spill on the Ecology in the Santa Barbara Channel?" *Biological and Oceanographical Survey of the Santa Barbara Oil Spill, 1969-71,* Allan Hancock Foundation, University of Southern California, 1971, Vol. I, Chap. 18, p. 401.

[13]*Sports Illustrated,* May 11, 1970, p. 19.

The way the lines look now, state, county and local governments and injured private parties will confront Union Oil, its three partners in the Santa Barbara Channel drilling venture — Mobil Oil Corp., Gulf Oil Corp., and Texaco, Inc. — and the U.S. government which set and supervised drilling regulations for the well.

A $1.3 million damage suit already has been filed against the four companies by representatives of Santa Barbara fishing and boating industries, beachfront property owners, and the beach-using public. The city of 70,000 residents draws an estimated $46 million a year from tourism, 80% of its livelihood. And the state of California may sue for violation of its water pollution, fish and game, and navigation laws.[14]

The Cumulative Effect

It is difficult to consider the Santa Barbara spill without expanding the analysis into other related areas. These areas include the American lifestyle, transportation, growth, and the energy crisis. These topics, outside the more limited topic of oil pollution, will be treated in later chapters. However, the Santa Barbara incident, tragic as it may be, is only a miniscule part of a massive and cumulative problem — oil pollution.

The term ecology, by its very definition, implies systemic relationships. Everything in our environment is related in some way to everything else. Nowhere is this more evident than in the seas. The effects of ecological disaster can be and are transmitted by winds, currents, and migratory species. While the injury caused by any one event may be localized, widespread but frequent occurrence of environmental damage may spread and accumulate with devastating synergistic effects. International oil pollution may be approaching this dimension today. Certainly the continued expansion and frantic search for oil is setting the stage for even greater disasters.

Consider the following:

1. The *Torrey Canyon,* considered a "supertanker" when it split and spilled its thirty-million gallon oil cargo into the sea 15 miles off England, would now be only a medium-sized ship. Tankers of over 200,000 tons deadweight are common; ships of 500,000 tons are being designed, and oil carriers of the future may be one million tons. The wreck of one tanker of 200,000 tons would equal the total tonnage of all tankers lost at sea from 1958 to 1968.[15]

2. Tankers will continue to increase in number. By 1983, about 4,300 such ships may be plying the seas. Total bulk-carrying vessels (including tankers) is forecast to increase from 17,369 in 1966 to 21,468 in 1983.[16] As the world grows smaller, so do the seas. Furthermore, this increasing traffic is concentrated in shipping lanes and ports. In the approximate

[14]*Business Week,* February 15, 1969, p. 30.
[15]Julian McCaull, "The Black Tide," *Environment,* November 9, 1969, pp. 2-3.
[16]McCaull, p. 3.

period between 1958 and 1968, 488 registered U.S. tankers of over 30 gross tons were involved in 553 collisions, and 472 (83%) of these collisions occurred as the ships were entering port.[17]

3. Harbors around the world are being enlarged to handle the super oil tankers of today and tomorrow.

4. At England's newest and most modern port, Milford Haven (bordered by a national park), three serious pollution episodes occurred during the first eight years of operation. At least 800 tons of oil entered the water. In 1967, 52 episodes of pollution were recorded ranging in spills from ten gallons to one ton.[18]

5. Prior to recent operational changes and restrictions, tankers dumped an estimated 1.5 million tons of oil into the sea annually as they flushed their tanks.[19]

6. Drilling and exploration is under way in the offshore waters of 50 countries. The pollution potential is not only related to blowouts. The dumping of oil-soaked drilling muds, oil storage, transfer, and transport all offer pollution potential. In 1969, there were an estimated 12,000 wells offshore along the coasts of Louisiana, Texas, California, and Alaska.[20] Offshore drilling is expanding at an increasing rate. The oil-bearing potential of the Santa Barbara Channel alone is sobering: " 'This latest leak makes it apparent that companies just can't control their wells,' says George Clude, chairman of the Santa Barbara County Board of Supervisors. 'There's a potential of 2000 to 4000 wells out off this coast and the people feel it's inevitable that something like this is going to happen again unless the drilling is stopped.' "[21]

Offshore production technology continues to advance. A new complex has been completed 58 miles offshore from the Arab state of Dubai. This new production site was discovered in 1966 and has been named the "Fateh Field." A new storage technology makes Fateh a prime example of advancing oil technology. Huge oil storage tanks known as "Khoyans," shaped like inverted funnels, have been built and sunk to the sea floor. The three tanks, 205 feet high, rest on the bottom in 158 feet of water with the tops and their service platforms projecting about 40 feet above the surface. Each tank holds 500,000 barrels of oil (about 27,500,000 gallons) and costs $8.5 million. The tanks, combined with the two Arab surface vessels, give the Fateh Field an offshore storage capacity of over two million barrels.[22]

The Oil/Government Conspiracy

The outlook for strict federal control over oil and protection of our

[17]McCaull, p. 3.   [18]McCaull, p. 4.   [19]McCaull, p. 4.
[20]*Business Week,* February 15, 1969, p. 31.
[21]*Newsweek,* June 16, 1969, p. 60.
[22]*Oceans,* July-August 1973, pp. 50-51.

environment is pessimistic. Government has long given oil "favorite son" treatment and regulatory exemptions. Why? Oil interests pay billions of dollars to the federal government for leasing rights. Government also earns royalties on production. In the Santa Barbara case, the government earns 16⅔% of market price for every barrel produced. Early estimates placed the reserves of the California tidelands at a conservative 4 billion barrels. Given these vast sums and the vested interest of oil, our offshore environment and coastal lands may not have a chance. Tens of thousands of Santa Barbara residents simply don't trust government and oil. The support of GOO's efforts clearly evidence this distrust. Oil and government have been openly described as liars who don't give a damn about Santa Barbara's ecology. The following arguments, among others, have been made.[23]

1. After great speeches concerning the tragic nature of the spill, Interior Secretary Hickel authorized drilling to be resumed on five federal channel leases only two months after the blowout. Hickel stated that he had been assured that this will be done with minimum threat to the environment. Approximately six weeks before Hickel's "reassuring" statement, a Union Oil vice-president had stated that no engineer could ever claim that there would not be a new spill.

2. In spite of the fact that he had declared Santa Barbara a disaster area, Governor Reagan would not support efforts to have the Santa Barbara drilling permanently discontinued and the platforms dismantled. Claims of a government/oil conspiracy were not weakened when Reagan appointed an Atlantic Richfield Oil Company employee as Director of the State Department of Fish and Game.[24]

3. Oil's influence with government is evident when the lack of policing is considered:

> The revenues to the Federal treasury from continental shelf leasing, plus royalties, have been running into hundreds of millions of dollars annually. It would take only a tiny percent of this amount to field and equip a force of tough inspectors and enforcement officers — men working for the public, not the oil companies — and to make the industry shape up.[25]

When Humble Oil wells in the Gulf of Mexico were inspected carefully, approximately 150 wells were in violation of safety regulations. Humble had claimed that all its offshore wells met safety requirements.

4. The oil/government conspiracy may have been directly responsible for the blowout considering the jealously guarded federal power and the fact that well A-21 was given a variance in safety regulation.

[23]Huglin, p. 66.
[24]Easton, pp. 66-67.
[25]*Audubon*, March 1969, p. 5.

Energy Versus Ecology 61

Once exploration began, two other Interior divisions clashed — the Federal Water Pollution Control Administration and the Oil and Gas Supervisor of the United States Geological Survey. California's chief deputy attorney general, Charles A. O'Brien, told the Senate subcommittee on air and water pollution during hearings in Santa Barbara: "The attitudes of these two Interior agencies is clearly explained by their titles — one is interested in pollution and the other is interested in oil. At a joint meeting of these agencies, which was attended by a California water control agency — the Oil and Gas Supervisor refused to allow either the federal or state water pollution experts any controls over the off-shore drilling operations. The Gas and Oil Supervisor not only refused to allow the promulgation of pollution regulations, he refused to allow any inspection of oil drilling operations by state or federal pollution experts." The Supervisor, D. W. Solanas, admitted that inspectors from his own office did not examine Union Oil well A-21 before it blew out. State officials testified that they would never have permitted a well to be drilled with less than 1200 feet of casing. Mr. Solanas granted a variance that allowed Union Oil to use only 230 feet of casing in order to extract oil from shallow sands. John Fraser of Union Oil said that more casing probably would have prevented the blowout.[26]

5. In an odd twist, the university was accused of being part of the oil/government team.

> Noting that his office had been unable to get assistance from petroleum experts from California universities, Deputy Attorney General stated, "The university experts all seem to be working on grants from the oil industry. There is an atmosphere of fear. The experts are afraid that if they assist us in our case on behalf of the people of California, they will lose their oil industry grants."[27]

6. The oil industry and the federal government had the money and the staying power to minimize the disaster in the minds of the American people. Oil wanted no threat to its preferred national position, and government wanted oil and the revenues that exploration and production bring. The strategy with which the spill was managed is further cause for pessimism.[28]

a. The pseudo-events. These included freezing out local control over Channel drilling, President Nixon's "personal inspection" of the disaster area (a beach that had been cleaned prior to his arrival), and legislative hearings that allowed locals to blow off steam but produced no action.

b. The creeping event. Under this strategy, nothing appears to be taking place. Events are programmed at a gradual and piecemeal pace. This prevents some of the consequences of detection and opposition that would occur if a major single event were perceived as happening. The gradual resumption of drilling provides an excellent example. Various wells were

---

[26]S. V. Roberts, *New Republic*, March 15, 1969, pp. 13-14.
[27]Molotch, pp. 48-49.   [28]Molotch, pp. 49-50.

put back into production in February and March. Drilling of new wells was gradually resumed and announced from April through August. The creeping event strategy does not provide a specific date worthy of massive news coverage and public attention.

c. The neutrality of science. Recruitement of university experts and scientists who are paid for their services with oil industry money gave a false air of finality and objectivity to postspill investigations.

d. Superficiality of the media. Events that are complex, scientific, and have long-term implications are not the meat of mass media. Investigative reporting is only beginning to become established. While the media give the short-term spotlight to ecological disasters, public attention is soon focused on some "new" event and forces seeking to mobilize public action soon see interest wane.

e. Routinization of evil. By routinizing undesirable events, the public builds a tolerance that can have dire consequences.

> Finally, perhaps the most pernicious technique of all because of damage it does to the social conscience, is the routinization of evil. Pollution of the Santa Barbara Channel is now routine; the issue is not whether or not the Channel is polluted, but *how much* it is polluted. A recent oil slick dismissed by an oil company official as a "routine" drilling by-product which was not viewed as "obnoxious." That about half of the oil currently seeping into the Channel is allegedly being recovered is taken as an improvement sufficient to preclude the "outrage" that a big national story would require.[29]

Get Oil Out.

Alvin Weingand, President of GOO, made an impassioned plea that summarized the frustration and fear of many citizens.

> The oil industry is like a caricature of a fat cat in a Herblock cartoon, grown so paunchy with unrestrained excesses that his credibility gap is showing.
>
> As a former State Senator I have come to respect the will of the people. I think the big polluting industries have had their way so long they feel they no longer have to pay attention to the simplistic and inarticulate warnings of popular discontent.
>
> Oilmen should listen to the simple instinctive cry of a child who gets oil in his hair on a Santa Barbara beach. There is more wisdom in it for the survival of man than in all the silver tongues on Madison Avenue, or all the incomplete science of Dale Straughan.
>
> Do the oil people think Cousteau is pulling their legs? Do they think Dr. Gordon MacDonald is just trying to spoil their breakfast when he says on the morning news that if we carry on paving the surface of the earth, the earth will die? Doesn't the President of Moneybags Oil Company have children or grandchildren, as the rest of us have? I sometimes wonder.
>
> Gentlemen, you must find a way out before our scientific advances ruin

[29]Molotch, p. 50.

the planet. The enjoyments of technology are like good whiskey, very nice in moderation, but too much will make you sick — and eventually kill you.[30]

Get Oil Out? No!

There are several excellent reasons why oil should continue to be sought and extracted from the Santa Barbara Channel and from coastal fields in general. The attitude of people who would simply shut off the energy switch in blind allegiance to erroneous ecological logic is reflected in the following statement:

> We find people denouncing papermills while consuming ever-increasing quantities of paper; driving their cars all over the country to berate the petroelum industry; burning electricity at meetings to upbraid the power industry; getting up in the morning, drinking a glass of Florida orange juice and denouncing the conversion of swamplands into orchards. They keep demanding more and more uses of their natural resources while demanding that they be left untouched. And your political leaders and public agencies are put in the intolerable position of being asked to heed simultaneously the demands expressed by the public in meeting-halls and indignation-meetings on the one hand, and the largely contradictory demands made by that same public in the marketplace and the employment bureau and the obstetrical ward on the other hand — because too many people have not considered the full implication of the courses they endorse.[31]

Why should oil stay? Let's examine several basic reasons.

"Better Them Than Us." It is ironic that California, particularly Southern California, should want to get oil out. Californians, with their penchant for mobility and independence, need oil. Each day they consume more. What is wrong here is that Californians are not against oil, they simply want all the benefits of energy without being bothered with the inconveniences. In a recent national television program residents of other coastal oil-producing states made no attempt to hide their contempt for this "let them drill someplace else" attitude.[32] There are two dimensions to this attitude, aesthetic and economic.

Aesthetic. The retired rich of Santa Barbara want their paradise preserved. No one can blame them for this. They also want their centrally air-conditioned homes at 70 degrees year-round, the unrestricted use of all their appliances, their wardrobes to look current with synthetic fabrics, their cars and other vehicles to be ready to go at a moment's notice, and their boats ready for fishing, cruising, or plain speeding around the Chan-

[30] Alvin C. Weingand, "The Santa Barbara Offshore Oil Case: Facts and Issues," in *Contemporary Challenges in the Business-Society Relationship*, George Steiner, ed. Graduate School of Management, UCLA, January, 1972. Chap. 14, pp. 11-12.

[31] Lt. Gen. Frederick T. Clarke, Chief of Engineers, U.S. Army, *The Wall Street OIRNAL*, April 27, 1970, p. 14.

[32] "The Energy Crisis," an N.B.C. three-hour television special aired September 4, 1973.

nel. No reasonable person would argue that offshore oil platforms add scenic beauty to the Santa Barbara Channel. But would the 70,000 people living in Santa Barbara be ultimately willing to discontinue using oil and oil-related products so that offshore exploration and drilling could be stopped?

Economic. As inflation continues to erode purchasing power new methods to reduce energy costs or retard its rate of increase are vitally needed. One such method is to supply regional energy needs from regional sources where a region is fortunate enough to have its own energy reserves. California is an excellent example of this potential. The oil needs of the state and region might be more economically supplied as local reserves are developed and utilized. Prices could remain lower as transportation expenses are reduced. New York faces a similar situation. Vast offshore oil potential exists off Long Island. Because ecologists have been successful in their efforts to prevent drilling and production off the coastline, New York City "imports" its natural gas supply from the 2,000-mile-distant Gulf Coast and scrambles for its supply of oil. The stubborn unwillingness of coastal states to develop their own resources places an unfair economic burden on their people and their region at the same time when resources needed by all continue to increase in price.

To Whom Does Oil Belong?

The argument that Santa Barbarans have the exclusive right to decide what will and will not be done with their offshore reserves is both provincial and selfish. It is analagous to forbidding the population of Los Angeles to breathe on days when the wind currents bring fresh air north from San Diego. The citizens of San Diego would, of course, claim that Los Angeles was now wrongly breathing San Diego air. To whom does oil belong? To everyone.

We recognize that the owner of property vital to public necessity has every legal right to be compensated for the use of his resource. States receive leasing, rental, and production payments from oil companies in return for the right to explore and extract. The federal government is similarly compensated for activities in its offshore waters. These payments represent major sources of needed income. Tax burdens are lightened and private employment is provided. Certainly any owner of property on land or offshore has the right to be justly compensated for its use. What about the moral right to approve its use in matters involving public necessity?

We Need Oil

Only the very few would argue the fact that we need oil. The residents of Santa Barbara didn't manufacture oil and store it under the Channel. It is a resource of nature. As such it belongs to our society as a whole. Does it make sense to close schools in Denver because there is no oil to warm the classrooms so that Santa Barbarans can continue to enjoy their view? The federal government resumed drilling and production off Santa Barbara in recognition of what was best for the nation. It is unfortunate when reality strikes at home, but energy is now too vital a resource to be withheld to satisfy a few.

An Industry Representative Speaks

In analyzing objections to oil's presence in the Channel and continued Channel development, Humble Oil's Western Division Exploration Manager Crandall Jones identified three common themes: "Why don't we go elsewhere in the United States to find oil?... If that is not feasible, why don't we import it?... If oil is vital to our national security, why not leave Santa Barbara oil in the ground as a reserve for the future?"[33] Mr. Jones' responses to these questions are summarized in the following paragraphs.

   1. Go elsewhere — We can't. Oil is where you find it based on geologic conditions, not human desire. Most of the offshore fields have now been discovered. With the exception of Alaska new discoveries are nil. The new supplies will come from under the waters of the continental shelves. In the 10 years from 1959 to 1969 inland reserves, excluding Alaska, declined 4 billion barrels. Offshore reserves, however, increased almost 2 billion barrels. Today over 17% of our domestic oil and 15% of our natural gas comes from offshore wells. Oilfields are simply too scarce to permit the luxury of abandoning the Santa Barbara Channel. Even the Alaskan reserves will not fill the gap between supply and demand.

   2. Shift to imports — We have, and we are becoming more and more dependent on foreign sources. By 1985 Humble Oil estimates that U.S. energy needs will double. By that time the United States will have to depend on foreign sources for over 60% of its oil. [Note: the author has seen later estimates as high as 70 plus %.] Who are these foreign suppliers? Largely the middle eastern countries and North Africa. Our political and diplomatic relationships with the Arab states particularly place us in a very precarious position. We face interrupted supply and uncertain prices. The U.S. must maintain capacity to cover interruptions in foreign supply and to have some ability to control short term prices. The only answer is to find more oil at home.

   3. Make Santa Barbara an oil reserve — We need oil, we need oil now, and we need Santa Barbara oil now. Even if it were possible to sit on reserves it takes several years to develop producing capacity. We are experiencing an energy crisis requiring increasing rates of oil consumption (the U.S. consumes about 17 million barrels of oil daily). Alternative energy sources simply can't fill the gap. Problems of radiation danger and thermal pollution have retarded the development of nuclear power. More stringent air pollution and mine safety laws have constrained the use of coal. Coal is also facing a tough battle with ecologists. Natural gas is already in short supply. The one source which must be supplemented to balance our nation's energy demands is oil.[34]

[33]Crandall Jones, "The Santa Barbara Offshore Oil Case: Facts and Issues," Steiner, Chap. 15, p. 7.

[34]Jones, pp. 7-9.

Jones summarizes his discussion of the question concerning alternatives to Santa Barbara:

> These are questions that are not confined to the Santa Barbara situation alone. All over the nation we are coming to grips with the central issue involved: how to provide for the needs of an expanding population and maintain the nation's economic health, while at the same time meeting rising expectations for an improved quality of life, environmentally and aesthetically.[35]

Oil's Ecological Effect — Major or Minor?

The initial reactions to the A-21 blowout and subsequent spill were a mixture of helplessness, fear, panic, anger, and sorrow. These attitudes were flavored with a high degree of emotion — even passion. These feelings were based, in part, on a fear of the ecological consequences resulting from the spill. The accident was billed as an ecological "disaster" by some and an "environmental crime" by others. Certainly the rapid release of oil into the Channel produced many undesirable effects. The most visible of these was the fouling of beaches, the harbor, and its vessels. Undeniably tragic was the death of shorebirds. The birds were lost but the beaches, harbor, and vessels were brought back into condition by massive and costly oil company clean-up efforts. The Santa Barbara visitor of today finds no major change in the Santa Barbara he enjoyed before the spill. But what about the unseen flora and fauna that depended on the Channel waters and intertidal zones as a life supporting ecosystem?

On February 20, 1969, the Allan Hancock Foundation, University of Southern California, received a research grant that was to answer this question. The grant was to cover the costs of a one-year field study to determine the immediate effects and shed light on possible long-term effects of the spill on Channel ecology.

> The opportunity for science to seek the answer came from a most logical source, the oil industry. While the oil was still on the water, Western Oil & Gas Association provided $240,000 in a no-strings-attached grant to the Allan Hancock Foundation at the University of Southern California. With origins dating back 60 years, the Hancock foundation had administered impartial academic research to the earth's polar waters and all the seas between.
>
> The foundation accepted the oil grant with firm understanding that the study would begin immediately, that the oil industry would exercise no influence, and that the findings would be published. Guidance for the study was charged to a committee of federal, state and private natural scientists.[36]

---

[35] Jones, p. 11.

[36] Don Dedera, "Santa Barbara, Alive and Well," *The Humble Way,* third quarter, 1971, pp. 2-3.

What did the scientists conclude?[37] Summarizing the findings of her scientist colleagues, Project Director Dr. Dale Straughan states:

1. There is no evidence of gross effects of oil pollution of plankton in the Santa Barbara Channel.[38]

2. Studies of the sandy beach fauna did not reveal any direct effects of oil pollution.[39]

3. Neither Neushul nor Nicholson and Cumbery were able to demonstrate widespread effect of oil production from the January, 1969, oil spill on intertidal species.[40]

4. Data presented on fish catches in the area and surveys by the California Department of Fish and Game suggest that the oil did not deplete the fish population and that the fishing industry suffered economic losses more through indirect causes such as the closing of harbor and fouling of boats and equipment.[41]

5. Relative to the seal, whale, and dolphin population, Dr. Straughan stated: "Data on the marine mammal populations do not prove large scale mortality as a result of the oil spill."[42]

6. A high mortality rate was recorded in pelagic bird populations. Only a very low percentage (10.7%) of all birds taken to cleaning centers survived.[43]

Dr. Straughan opened her summary by stating: "First, we do not know all the answers — we will probably never know all of the answers."[44] She closed by saying: "In conclusion, I would like to reiterate that damage to the biota was not widespread, but was limited to several species, and that the area is recovering. In retrospect it is not surprising that the studies after the Santa Barbara oil spill revealed such a small amount of damage. However, recurrent spills of this type at frequent intervals would probably result in large ecological changes. Likewise, spills of refined oils present an entirely different problem and one that warrants far more concern."[45]

The results published by the Hancock Foundation scientists were considerably different that those prophesied by GOO and others critical of oil's Santa Barbara presence.

> These results are not easily accepted by many Americans. Millions had judged the Santa Barbara spill to be an ecological disaster of first magnitude. Understandably so; from what they saw, heard and read, they assumed the Santa Barbara Channel might become a "marine desert" and "dead sea." Furthermore, press coverage of the spill was intense. Stories told of numerous stranded whales, oil-suffocated seals "as far as the eye could see," a devastated fishery, and tidal zones and beaches hopelessly stripped of life.

---

[37]See Dale Straughan, Vols. I and II, for a complete report on the investigation and findings. [38]Straughan, p. 401. [39]Straughan, p. 403. [40]Straughan, p. 405.
[41]Straughan, p. 410. [42]Straughan, p. 41. [43]Straughan, p. 411. [44]Straughan, p. 401.
[45]Straughan, p. 417. (Author's note: The toxic effect of crude oil is much less severe and persistent than that of refined oil such as heating fuel or diesel oil.)

Not even a five-million-dollar cleanup was given much credit for restoration of the coast. Santa Barbara became the battle cry of the Age of Ecology.[46]

Sponsored researchers are always subject to accusations that they have failed to fully disclose findings which were not favorable to their sponsors.

Those who have questioned the integrity of Hancock scientists quicken Dr. Straughan's Aussie temper, which includes a few houshold cuss words. "I don't know how to cope with that kind of attack," said she. "I tell things as I see them. I don't have to defend myself."

But it has hurt her deeply that some who disagree with the Hancock study have accused her of not caring about the environment.

"Of course I care about my environment," she said. "Part of the public conclusion is based on an erroneous assumption that all oil spills are the same. Yet a Santa Barbara is not a *Tampico Maru*, and a *Falmouth* is not a *Torrey Canyon*. It happens that Santa Barbara crude is a heavy oil, relatively insoluble in water, and low in toxic fractions."

She continued, "It's obvious to me that one, single spill is sort of the least of our worries. Not that I mean oil pollution research is unimportant. Otherwise, I wouldn't be doing it. But it must be kept in perspective with other pollution — by chemicals, sewage, heavy metals, heat, pesticides, and radioactivity."[47]

Santa Barbara, Part of a Bigger Issue

T. D. Barrow, president of Humble Oil and Refining Company, believes the management of coastal zones to be one of the most important issues facing our nation. He states that while coastal waters and submerged lands are largely publicly owned, it has been private development that has enhanced their economic value and productivity. Barrow suggests that:

> ...the federal government could review state plans for managing coastal zones to assure that these plans are consistent with the national interests. Implementation of the plans should be left to state and local governments and private interests. Financial assistance could be provided to the states from the federal level. The federal government would also, obviously, operate within the coastal zones in matters such as coastal defense, immigration and customs.
>
> But the real focal points for coastal zone management should be at the state level.[48]

Is oil an either/or proposition? No. We do not have the luxury of considering the question. Should we continue to permit oil in the Channel, or get oil out? Certainly the Santa Barbara spill was tragic, damaging, inconvenient, and expensive for all concerned. In fact, no one can guarantee with 100% certainty that offshore oil will not again be spilled any more than the airline industry can guarantee 100% that no accidents will occur.

[46]Dedera, p. 2.   [47]Dedera, pp. 6-7.

[48]T. D. Barrow, "Private Property and the Coastal Zones," *The Humble Way*, third quarter, 1971, p. 25.

The question is really one of making man's needs as compatible with the environment as possible. Barrow continues:

> State and local planning activity should be based on the fundamental principle of compatible use. By "compatible use," I mean a flexible framework of use priority for coastal lands and waters. This should be a dynamic rather than a static concept. It should recognize the unique characteristics of each area of coastal lands or waters — whether these characteristics be esthetic, biological, or economic. It should recognize the possible preeminent uses of these lands or waters, based on their characteristics. And it should not predetermine that one land or water use will always be desirable — nor another use always undesirable.
>
> Flexibility — in law, in administration, in philosophy — will bring great dividends to the nation in the management of its coastal zones.[49]

Summarizing the complex Santa Barbara case from the oil industry point of view is not an easy task. Often, however, simplicity is the best way to deal with complexity. A statement by Crandall Jones gets to the nut of the issue:

> Some would have us believe that economic progress and conservation of nature are mutually exclusive objectives, that we must choose between one and the other. I do not. I believe that we can reach both these objectives. We in the petroleum industry know that if we are allowed to develop the Santa Barbara Channel we shall inevitably be damned by *some:* but if the nation runs short of oil we would be damned by *all*.[50]

Postscript

It is vital that you reflect carefully on both sides of the Santa Barbara dispute. In the next 10 to 15 years, and possibly further into the future, the issues of Santa Barbara will be replayed again and again. There will be even greater urgency and crescendo. In addition to the problems associated with Alaskan oil and the current oil shortage, the entire offshore East Coast of the United States is up for grabs. The several states involved fight desperately to keep oil out as the federal government attempts to seek the correct path between the problem of energy and environment. Oil has recently been found off Nova Scotia. This Canadian province already has extensive refining, storage, and transport capabilities. Canada estimates up 25 billion barrels of reserves off its Atlantic shores. The U.S. coast appears equally promising along its entire length. Reserves of perhaps 40 billion barrels may exist in three major areas:

> The Georges Bank, roughly 14,000 square miles lying southeast of Cape Cod, where ocean bottom sediments are believed to be favorable for oil deposits.

[49]Barrow, p. 26.
[50]Jones, p. 11.

The Baltimore Canyon Trough, an area of about 12,000 square miles off New York, New Jersey, Delaware and Maryland, where some of the thickest — and possibly most favorable — geologic formations for oil occur.

The Blake Plateau, more than 60,000 square miles stretching offshore from Cape Hatteras south to Florida. The plateau, a gently sloping portion of the continental shelf, is the largest prospective area for oil and gas — but also the most difficult because it lies in deep water as much as 200 miles offshore.

"The estimates of reserves in these areas are highly speculative," says Shell Oil's Senior Staff Geologist William R. Cobb.

"But when you're talking about the possibility of 40 billion barrels of oil, it's worth going after — even when it's speculative."[51]

New decisions concerning offshore oil operations will be made in the next five to ten years. What should we do?

Discussion Questions

1. a. Who was to blame for the Santa Barbara oil spill?
   b. What support do you offer for fixing the blame(s)?
2. a. Specifically, what measures do you think could have been taken, short of banning Channel oil exploration and production, to prevent the spill?
   b. Why were these measures not taken?
3. Evaluate the following statements:
   a. "Oil spent 5 million dollars, countless man hours, and took considerable physical risk in stopping and cleaning up the spill. No one even said thank you. People act like we wanted this accident to occur!"
   b. "Thanking the oil industry for cleaning up the horrible mess it caused at Santa Barbara is like thanking an axe murderer for cleaning up the blood!"
4. a. Do you accept the findings of the Hancock Foundation scientific team? Why or why not?
   b. How do you feel about the integrity of the researchers after learning that they were sponsored ($240,000) by an oil industry trade association?
   c. Who should be assigned investigative responsibility in such cases? How should their work be funded? Would you (private citizen/taxpayer) pay for it?
5. Discuss the "credibility gap" that was alleged to have existed between industry spokesmen and local government.
   a. In what specific instances were there differences in facts?
   b. What differences in attitudes appeared to exist?
   c. Is there a better system for controlling the analysis and reporting of complex events that have high emotional overtones? Be specific concerning feasible improvements.
6. Concerning news media coverage of the spill:
   a. Are there any industry (broadcast and print media) codes that govern reporting?
   b. What do such codes prescribe?

[51]*The Miami Herald*, September 10, 1973, p. 24-A.

c. In what ways did the media act as a positive force during and after the incident?
   d. In what ways were the media a negative force?
7. Concerning offshore resources:
   a. Who should control the use of offshore waters and submerged lands? Why?
   b. Is a 3-mile limit sufficient for meaningful state control?
   c. What criteria would you apply in classifying an offshore resource as a national necessity?
8. Assume that the Santa Barbara spill had resulted from the collision of two oil tankers carrying number 2 diesel oil.
   a. Would the ecological effect in channel waters and intertidal areas have been the same?
   b. Specifically what difference would you predict? Why?
9. a. How do you react to the alleged "conspiracy" between the federal government and Santa Barbara oil interests?
   b. Can you cite specific evidence to support or refute this allegation?
10. Assume you had the power to draft a U.S. energy policy for the remainder of the twentieth century. What would you recommend? Why?
11. On January 25, 1970, in a CBS interview on "Face the Nation," Walter T. Hickel, then Secretary of the Interior, stated: "The polluters will have to pay. It will be a cost of doing business." There are at least three basic approaches to paying for pollution control:
   a. The pollutor "absorbs" the cost.
   b. All costs are reflected in increased consumer prices.
   c. Government assists business by funding research, providing technology, giving tax incentives, etc.
   Which of these approaches do you favor? Why?
12. How do you feel concerning the use of underwater oil storage tanks? What safeguards exist? What dangers exist?

Suggested Class Projects

1. a. Develop a list of several recent oil pollution incidents other than Santa Barbara.
   b. From your list select an open sea incident and an inland river or harbor incident.
   c. Develop data concerning the incidents you have selected.
   d. Prepare a comparative analysis of the similarities and differences between the Santa Barbara Channel spill and the other two selected.
   e. What conclusions and recommendations are suggested by your work?
2. a. List and describe oil spill clean-up techniques.
   b. Rate each technique on at least four dimensions:
      monetary cost
      effectiveness
      availability (how soon it can be mobilized?)
      side effects
   c. What conclusions and recommendations do you reach?

d. Comment about current research into spill clean-up technology.
3. a. Secure copies of the National Multiagency Oil and Hazardous Materials Contingency Plan and any later materials that may have amended or superceded it.
b. Obtain copies of your local area's contingency plan.
c. Analyze these plans and prepare a written critique.
4. Several panel presentations are possible. After studying the Santa Barbara case your group could form any of the following panels:
a. Oil industry (company and/or trade association representatives) panel to present a discussion of energy needs and offshore drilling.
b. Secure Union Oil's film concerning Santa Barbara. Have it shown by a company representative who will lead a subsequent discussion.
c. Invite local, regional, or national pollution control and environmental officials to discuss governmental regulation and control.
5. How aware and concerned is the public relative to offshore oil issues?
a. Conduct a survey in your area to attempt to measure knowledge and attitudes concerning offshore oil and related issues.
b. Refer to basic marketing research textbooks for guidelines concerning project planning, sampling techniques, questionnaire design, tabulation of data, report preparation, etc. (Remember, your survey results are only as good as your research methodology.)
c. Based on your results, answer question number 4. What next steps need to be taken to correct gaps in information?
d. Based on this initial effort, what additional research would you recommend?

Supplementary Readings

Books

Biological and Oceanographical Survey of Santa Barbara Oil Spill. Vols. I, II. Santa Barbara: Allan Hancock Foundation, University of Southern California, 1971.
Easton, Robert. *Black Tide: The Santa Barbara Oil Spill and Its Consequences.* New York: Delacorte Press, 1972.
Eco-Castrophe. New York: Harper & Row, 1970. A collection of essays selected by the editorial staff of *Ramparts*.
Marx, Wesley. *Oilspill.* San Francisco: Sierra Club, 1971.
Smith, I. E., ed. *Torrey Canyon, Pollution and Marine Life.* New York: Cambridge University Press, 1968.
Steiner, George A., ed. *Contemporary Challenges in the Business-Society Relationship.* Los Angeles: University of California Graduate School of Management, 1972. Particularly note part III.
Wulf, Norman A. *Contiguous Zones for Pollution Control: An Appraisal Under International Law.* Sea Grant Technical Bulletin No. 13. Coral Gables, Fla.: University of Miami Sea Grant Program, 1971.

Articles

"Another Oil Slick." *Newsweek,* February 24, 1969, p. 37.

"Big Oil Leak Leaves a Messy Legal Residue." *Business Week,* February 15, 1969, pp. 30-32.
"Black But Clear Lesson from Santa Barbara." *Audubon,* March 1969, p. 5.
"California Oil Strike Nobody Wanted." *Life,* February 14, 1969, pp. 30-31.
"Dead Channel." *Time,* February 21, 1969, p. 21.
"Effects of the Santa Barbara Blowout." *U.S. News and World Report,* February 8, 1971, p. 54.
"Fighting the Oil on California's Troubled Waters." *Business Week,* gfebruary 8, 1969, pp. 60-61.
"GOO and More GOO." *New Republic,* February 6, 1971, p. 14.
"GOO Story." *Newsweek,* June 16, 1969, p. 60.
"Helpless Birds, Helpless Technology." *Science,* February 22, 1969, pp. 183-184.
Huglin, T. "Diary of a Disaster: Santa Barbara Oil Slick." *McCalls,* June 1970, p. 58.
Kennedy, T. "Tarring and Feathering of Santa Barbara." *Motor Boating,* April 1969, pp. 60-61.
"A Khaozyn Named Dubai: Something New in Underwater Storage Facilities." *Oceans,* July-Aug. 1973, pp. 50-51.
McCaull, Julian, "The Black Tide." *Environment,* November 9, 1969, pp. 2-16.
Molotch, Harvey. "Oil in the Velvet Playground." *Ramparts,* November 1969, pp. 44-51.
"Nature Against Herself: Oil's Natural Pollution of the Sea." *Oceans,* July-Aug. 1973, pp. 34-38.
Roberts, S. V. "Oil Pressure; Conservationists vs. Interior Departments." *New Republic,* March 15, 1969, pp. 13-14.

5
The Unplanned Yet Inevitable Purchase

Linda enters the darkened room. She feels her mother's hand pressing hers. Mrs. Roan and Linda stand for a moment, adjusting to the new surroundings and light. Immediately, they notice it in the center of the room. It glows in the bright yet soft spotlight. Yes, this is the one they had heard about. This is the one they have read and talked about. Truly beautiful, truly elegant, truly regal, and clearly several cuts above the rest.

Where are Linda and Mrs. Roan? Have they entered a theater-in-the-round to see a play? Are they at a rock concert where the star performer has taken center stage? Perhaps at an auto show? What is the center of visual attention? A theater set? A rock star? The latest Ferrari? No — it's a casket.

Yes, the center of attention is a casket. Linda and Mrs. Roan are at the Winston Funeral Home and have just entered the casket showroom.

They carefully examine this product. The subtle beauty and individualistic workmanship create a dignified, yet warm, design. The skillful blending of rich woods and optional pearlescent and satin-sheen finish provide a difficult choice for the buyer seeking the finest. The simple yet eloquent, engraved ornamentation sets this model off from all others. However, as Mr. Winston has pointed out, the real difference is the interior. The cloud white and sky blue colors look restful. The interior appointments are lush, with the finest in elegant fabrics. Placed in the recommended protective vault, this product will provide lasting protection and eternal peace of mind for the discriminating.[1]

Mrs. Roan and her 19-year-old daughter, Linda, have suddenly become consumers in what most of us would call a unique purchasing situation. In reality, this situation is not unique at all. Death is a necessity of life. Each of you will one day be directly and perhaps suddenly involved in making one of life's largest cash purchases. In the next several pages, we will be living through this experience with Linda and Mrs. Roan. We will view this consumer/business interaction through the eyes of Mr. Roan's surviving family, as they experience it and as they reflect upon it. Equally as important, we will view this situation through the eyes of Mr. Roy Winston, the funeral director. You will be briefly exposed to his background and his professional philosophy of consumer service. Finally,

[1] This description combines terminology collected from several burial industry advertisements.

you will have the opportunity to analyze this consumer/business interface and be assisted in developing commentary and discussion by a series of questions, assignments, and supplementary readings.

To derive the greatest learning potential from this experience, you must first completely assume the identity of the consumers, Linda and her mother. Place yourself squarely in their circumstances. Imagine that you have experienced their sudden and saddening loss. This should not be difficult. Then switch identities. Assume the role of Mr. Winston, not just partially but as completely as possible. The degree to which you can meet the personal and individual challenge of role exchange will be in direct proportion to the insights, emotional empathy, desire for additional information, and excitement that true learning can bring. Of course, you will have a tendency to identify more with one party in the case than with the other. This is a temptation you must resist, a natural tendency you must fight against. As honestly as possible, attempt to assume each role. See the world through the eyes of each party. Then rethink and analyze both perspectives before developing your own viewpoint.

Unexpected Yet Inevitable

Mr. Roan was fifty-two on his most recent birthday. His health was excellent. Mrs. Roan, 47, and Linda, 19, were looking forward to their long awaited European camping trip. The Roans had saved for several years and had finally planned the trip for the coming summer. With Linda going off to college, this would probably be the last time they would take a family vacation together. They were planning to go all out. Then it happened. The phone call from Mr. Roan's office described it as an apparent heart attack. Mr. Roan was rushed to the nearest hospital. Mr. Roan was dead.

Mandatory Buyers of Unsought Goods

Marketing men have developed a taxonony that classifies all products according to the manner in which they are sought and purchased.[2] Suddenly, Linda and Mrs. Roan find themselves as mandatory consumers in the "unsought goods market." Unsought goods have the following characteristics:

1. Consumers see little current need to purchase or to plan for future purchases.

[2] Classification of Goods Theory is discussed in most marketing textbooks. The primary classifications are: convenience, shopping, specialty, and unsought goods. For complete summary of the theory and its applications, see E. Jerome McCarthy, *Basic Marketing, a Managerial Approach,* 4th ed. (Homewood, Illinois: Richard B. Irwin Inc., 1971), pp. 300-319.

2. Unsought products are often relatively expensive. For example, a set of encyclopedias for home use is not as expensive as a car but is expensive relative to other books.

3. Consumers may make a special effort to avoid thinking about and planning for purchases in the unsought market. Have you selected your burial plot? Have you planned for ambulance service?

4. Unsought goods are purchased infrequently.

5. Many unsought goods may be thought of as necessities when the need arises.

6. Personal selling is the major marketing mix ingredient.

7. There is little consumer search and comparison.

8. A consumer suddenly thrust into the unsought market may be vulnerable to impulse buying.

Why have we taken this brief side trip into Classification of Goods Theory? Because it is the very nature of unsought products and the way we behave as consumers in the unsought market that underpin the Roan's situation. Are the Roans at an undue disadvantage as consumers in the unsought market? If so, who is to blame? What part does impulse and emotion play in the purchase of unsought products?

The purchasing decisions concerning services for Mr. Roan are simultaneously unplanned and immediate. One of the first questions asked by the hospital staff after Mr. Roan arrives is, "Who is your funeral director?" The Roans have only recently settled in their new city and have no "family funeral director." Mrs. Roan asks hospital personnel and her neighbor, who has accompanied her, for their recommendations. Based on these brief discussions the decision is made to use the nearby Winston Funeral Home. Mr. Winston's ambulance arrives promptly and transfers the remains to his establishment. Mr. Winston then calls Mrs. Roan. An appointment is scheduled for Mrs. Roan to visit the Winston Funeral Home the following afternoon.

You might consider it maudlin or cruel to discuss Linda's and Mrs. Roan's emotional state in any detail. Yet, how they feel and act during this experience will have a direct bearing on the type and cost of service purchased. Because of the emotional nature of this purchasing situation, the decision of the next afternoon may have a long-range effect on the Roan's postpurchase feelings as well. I'll simply trust you to identify with the Roans and experience the shock, the grief, and the depth of emotion they feel as they leave home and drive to the funeral home to enter into this important business transaction.

Mr. Winston greets the Roans as they enter his establishment. He immediately takes them to his office and makes them feel at ease. The office is tastefully yet conservatively furnished. Soft and soothing music serves as a background to the arrangements conference. The Roans are impressed by Mr. Winston's interest, understanding, helpfulness, and sincerity. Mr. Winston takes the initiative and outlines a recommended service. The service sounds beautiful and, for the first time, Mrs. Roan feels less depressed. Linda, however, has noted the richly appointed facility and expresses some concern over the cost of the funeral and related services. Mr. Winston states that he will be pleased to provide an estimate, but that he requires some additional decisions before he can discuss cost intelligently. In addition to certain details concerning the conduct of the services, Mr. Winston will need some decisions concerning the cemetery, the grave type, and the site. Also, casket selection will have to be made. At this point, Linda's apprehension mounts. The Roans are not a wealthy family. Most of their savings had gone into the new house following Mr. Roan's transfer. The expense and the unforeseen costs associated with moving has left the Roans in a poor cash position. Mr. Roan had only a modest amount of life insurance. Inflation had very severely reduced its true value over time. Linda thought: "If we only had more time — if we only had a chance to compare — if we only had a chance to talk over other alternatives." As Linda reflected on her feelings, Mr. Winston and her mother continued to discuss and settle the plans for the service.

Mr. Winston's discussion tactfully yet directly included the arrangements for paying the funeral bills. These questions were handled diplomatically and with a great deal of sensitivity. These were not pleasant matters yet they were facts that had to be faced. During the arrangements conference, Mr. Winston learned of Mr. Roan's life insurance policy. He also inquired concerning any burial benefits from Mr. Roan's lodge membership and wondered if Mr. Roan's company had any benefits that might help cover this burial expense. Mr. Winston reminded Mrs. Roan of the lump-sum Social Security benefit to which she was entitled. "It's not a great deal," he said, "but it will be a help." Mrs. Roan had not remembered the Social Security death benefit and felt somewhat relieved when Mr. Winston brought it to her attention. However, her primary throughts were still of her husband. His will contained no specific statement concerning burial costs or arrangements. And now several important, expensive, and final decisions were clearly up to Mrs. Roan.

As they entered the casket room, Mr. Winston quietly explained the benefits of his best models. He knew they would want the finest for Mr. Roan. Of course, the Roans asked to be shown additional caskets and carefully reviewed the literature concerning several models. However, it was obvious that the casket so prominently and beautifully displayed as they entered the selection room was Mrs. Roan's first preference. Linda felt uneasy about the cost — well over one thousand dollars. Mr. Winston, however, reinforced Mrs. Roan's preference. He stressed the guarantee, the lasting protection, the pride, and the peace of mind such a product would provide. This would indeed be a purchase that Mrs. Roan could take pride in and a gesture that her friends and family would appreciate. Mrs. Roan reflected only a moment, and the decision was made. Yes, the finest.

Diligently working behind the scenes, Mr. Winston arranged a complete and beautiful funeral. Mrs. Roan did the very best she could for her husband: the large viewing parlor, several viewing hours, complete services, prominent cemetery, high quality burial vault, perpetual lot care, and an impressive monument. One of Mr. Roan's lodge brothers remarked "I've never seen such a fine funeral. Jim really went out in style. Must have cost a bundle." It did.

Linda opened the envelope with the Winston Funeral Home return address. The invoice stated simply "For casket and services ... $1,825." During the next several days additional bills were received from the ambulance service, the hospital, the attending physician, the cemetery, and the monument company. These bills totaled over $950. There was no provision for or encouragement to make installment payments in any of the invoices. The $10,000 life insurance check they had received only days before seemed smaller. The following week the tuition and board statement for Linda's first year at the university arrived. It was close to $3,000.

As the days passed, Linda began to reflect on the brief but expensive stay as a consumer in the unsought market. Several questions entered her mind. If the family had had the opportunity to shop, as they did for other major purchases, could they have saved? Why did Mr. Winston ask about insurance and other benefits during the arrangements conference? Would a $400 casket have sufficed? Was a traditional funeral necessary at all? Couldn't the payments of the burial debts be spread out like the payments of other expensive purchases? Were the short-term benefits her mother received worth the long-term cost? Were the benefits her mother received short- or long-term? What would her father have really wanted — an elaborate and expensive funeral or greater financial security for his survivors? Had the salesmanship, display, and emotional vulnerability made them easy prey? Had they been "taken"?

Meet Roy Winston

Let's briefly examine Mr. Roy Winston's background and professional training. We will attempt to understand how he fits into this consumer/business equation. Is he a villian? We'll watch Mr. Winston as he speaks to a graduating mortuary science class at the local college. As you begin to gain an insight into his profession and philosophy, you will also gain a more balanced and realistic perspective of this economic transaction. With this balanced perspective you will be asked to consider several dimensions of this consumer/business interaction.

Roy Winston didn't always want to enter the funeral profession. But, the business built by his father was going well. Roy had helped his father from the time he was a small boy, and when he considered what to study in college, a career in mortuary science seemed the best decision. Roy studied for two years at junior college, majoring in the mortuary science curriculum. Soon after graduation, he became a licensed funeral director and gradually took full control of his father's business. He worked hard and eventually earned a degree in business administration as an evening student. Over the years Roy often thought about his work. As he saw it there were two distinct parts: first, the logistics of body movement, processing, and interment; and second, the personal services provided to those arranging the funeral — his clients. This second set of activities included arrangements for religious services, arranging for the clothing to be used, providing assistance at viewings, coordination with cemetery personnel, securing the additional services or products needed, such as burial vaults, comforting friends and relatives of the deceased, and, most important, providing a meaningful and beautiful ceremony that resulted in a therapeutic, grief-reducing experience for the widowed, bereaved family members, and friends. It is this latter part of his work that gave a professional designation to Mr. Winston's career and provided him with a large measure of self-satisfaction.

The Traditional Funeral, Culture, and the Consumer

The unsought purchase that strained the Roan's budget was a "traditional funeral." The traditional funeral is a service that includes:
1. Retention of a funeral director to plan and conduct services
2. Cosmetic preparation and dressing of the deceased
3. Use of casket and burial vault
4. Open viewing of the body
5. Religious services
6. Public display of sympathy through floral and other gifts[3]
7. Terrestrial internment

---

[3]An industry critic estimated that in 1960 approximately 65% of the floral industry's sales were for sympathy flowers. Jessica Mitford, *The American Way of Death* (New York: Simon & Schuster, 1963).

8. Emphasis on body preservation and protection through the use of a casket and burial vault[4]
9. Perpetual care of the grave site
10. Use of a monument to mark the grave

Mr. Winston's background, education, and experience have convinced him that the traditional funeral is the best product for most of his clients. His belief is genuine and sincere. True, the traditional funeral gives the funeral director the widest opportunity to provide service. The traditional funeral also holds the greatest profit potential. But what is wrong with this? A funeral director must earn a profit to remain in business and provide his services to the public.

Over the last few decades there has been evidence that some individuals prefer not to have the traditional funeral. Variations on the traditional funeral have included:

1. Cremation. Still insignificant nationally. The current cremation rate is about 4%. California presently has the highest rate, about 17%.[5]

2. Body donation. After minor preparation the body becomes the property of a medical school, teaching hospital, medical research organization, etc. Memorial services are held; however, the body is not present or is it part of any traditional service.

3. Burial cooperatives. Like all cooperatives these groups have been formed to give the buyer/member greater control. Through prearranging large numbers of funeral transactions cooperative members seek to reduce funeral costs and gain other benefits.

4. Cryonics. Preservation of the body by deep-freezing. The ultimate goal is to bring the corpse back to life when and if the technology is developed. This extremely expensive process received much initial publicity, but it has not become popular or even potentially popular. Some physicians feel that prolonged freezing causes irrevocable tissue damage.

In general, the only significant challenge to the traditional funeral is cremation. If there are less expensive and less involved ways to take care of the death situation, why has the traditional funeral endured? Why did the Roans purchase this product? Why will the majority of Americans experiencing the loss of a loved one purchase this staple of the funeral industry?

[4]A burial vault is a container placed inside the grave to hold and protect the casket from deterioration. Vaults are made of many materials, but the concrete vault is the most popular and economical. Cemetries often require the use of vaults. The basis for this requirement is that the vault provides a secure lining for the grave and prevents future problems caused by the shifting and settling of the earth.

[5]"Cremation In the United States," *The NCBVA Bulletin,* National Concrete Burial Vault Association, Inc., Harrisburg, Pa. (April, 1971), p. 2.

To gain additional insight concerning the traditional funeral we will sit in with an audience composed of a graduating junior college class in mortuary science. The graduates have invited Mr. Winston to deliver their commencement address. The following paragraphs contain his presentation. Much of Mr. Winston's personal philosophy is reflected in his remarks.

The traditional funeral is an American cultural ceremony. Throughout the ages, cultures have had specific ways in which they handle life's basic situations. These basic situations include birth, the reaching of maturity, marriage, and death. The traditional funeral has its basis in religion. The commitment of the deceased to God in the hope of spiritual resurrection and eternal life. The traditional funeral also has secular implications. The needs of the living are as important as the needs of the dead. The funeral ceremony permits the bereaved to adjust to and face the reality of death. The proper foundation for this psychological adjustment is vital to the mental well-being of the bereaved. Throughout recorded civilization various cultures have had one thing in common, the use of ceremony and public ventilation of grief at the time of death. These rites existed long before we knew anything about psychology and mental health. They existed because of an innate human need. Funeral ceremonies have continued to exist because they satisfy the basic needs of most societies. Both the spiritual need of the deceased and the emotional needs of the living have been served over centuries by the traditional funeral ceremony.

Mr. Winston continued by quoting from a recent article written by a prominent funeral industry executive. The article stated:

In general, a funeral service can be observed from four viewpoints.
The humanistic phase or the need to cope with death itself, and the fulfilling of the tasks necessary for the disposition of the body.
The societal phase in which the community or group gives support to bereaved.
The emotional adjustment of the bereaved in accepting the reality of death...
The relationship of the funeral ceremony to the theological and religious beliefs of the bereaved... The most satisfactory funeral would be that which, in addition to disposing of the body, also brings together group or community support for the bereaved, helps all to accept the reality of death, and gives meaning to man's relationship to God.
Beyond these broad definitions of the function and purpose of the funeral we might consider methods of evaluating a funeral service.
It should provide a means by which the family knows of the willingness of the community to share its loss. There should be every opportunity for the group to symbolize its respect for the memory of the deceased through the sending and the displaying of flowers.
The funeral should express an understanding of the social, fraternal, and religious relationships of the living to the deceased.
The funeral must assist the family in their recognition of the reality of death.

The funeral should offer an opportunity for the expression of feeling by the bereaved.

The funeral should enable the family to have access to all the religious sources for understanding loss and suffering.

The funeral should develop the perspective for the meaning of life and death in light of the contingency created by death.

The funeral should assist the family and the community to comprehend the nature of man and his relationship to God.[6]

Mr. Winston concludes his speech by citing a case example. The case involved a young girl and her mother planning burial services for the head of the family who died suddenly and unexpectedly well before his time.

"It is impossible to estimate the value of the lasting benefits to my client, her young daughter, relatives, and friends provided by the services," Mr. Winston stated.

As he closed this presentation to the funeral directors of the future he added:

> Our industry represents an unusual combination of a business and a profession. The business-related tasks are demanding. We have no hours and must be available for service 365 days a year, 24 hours a day. The work is physically and psychologically taxing. Often the work is also unpleasant. And yet, it is a job that must be performed in every society.
>
> On the other hand the professional aspects of your future career provide the opportunity and privilege of easing human pain and sorrow. Your clients put their trust in you to plan and conduct one of our society's most important cultural ceremonies. You will experience the lasting professional satisfaction of knowing that your career field is not only necessary but valuable to society. Approach each client with honesty and sincerity and always remember that the needs of the living must be served as well as the needs of the dead.

There was a long moment of silence as Mr. Winston returned to his seat. Each graduating student felt a sense of pride in his chosen work. As they each entertained private thoughts concerning the future, they especially looked forward to serving their fellow men.

---

[6]Ralph A. Head, "The Reality of Death," *Casket & Sunnyside* 101, No. 6 (June 1971), pp. 21-22.

Discussion Questions

1. Was Mrs. Roan justified in purchasing such an expensive service for her husband? Why? Why not?
2. Discuss Linda's postpurchase anxiety.
   a. How would you answer the questions Linda asks? What are the reasons underpinning your position?
   b. Why might Linda feel different than her mother about the purchase?
3. How do you feel about Mr. Winston's analysis of the total funeral product, i.e., the humanistic as well as the logistical services performed?
4. Is Mr. Winston wrong to promote the better items in his line? Why? Why not?
5. Assume that you now own the Winston Funeral Home. Would you make any changes in its marketing practice? Specifically, what changes?
6. Assume your sole income, profits from the Winston Funeral Home, has been diminishing. Would you attempt to increase sales? Profit? Specifically, how?
7. Considering the publicity given funeral industry critics over the years, why has the traditional funeral continued to represent the vast majority of funeral purchases?
8. Compare and discuss several of the comparative aspects of products in the unsought market. For example, what similarities and differences exist between the burial need purchase and the emergency need for legal representation or medical service.
9. Is the consumer at any inherent disadvantage in the unsought market?
   a. What are these disadvantages?
   b. Who is to blame?
   c. What steps do you recommend to change the situation?
10. What criteria would you use to define a "reasonable" price and profit in the burial industry?
11. What sort of burial services will you purchase? For others? For yourself?
12. State and analyze the reasons for your answer to number 11.
13. Should the burial industry be federally regulated? Elaborate concerning advantages and disadvantages to regulation for both society and business.

Suggested Class Projects

These assignments may be performed on an individual, project group, or class basis.

1. Develop a short questionnaire concerning the psychological and spiritual values of the traditional funeral. Interview behavioral scientists, physicians, and clergymen. Prepare a comparative analysis of the results. What conclusions can you reach?
2. a. Select an unsought product. Prepare a schematic model illustrating the actions and interactions of a typical consumer with the business organization. Your model should be complete, beginning with the consumer's characteristics and needs through to the postpurchase state. See texts in consumer behavior and marketing management for illustrations of consumer decision models.
   b. Compare your model for the unsought market to at least one consumer purchase model from the literature.

c. Analyze the differences.

3\. a. Develop a statistical and descriptive portrait of the burial industry today.

b. Based on this information develop a forecast of likely burial industry changes over the next 100 years. Your forecast should be based on current data plus the cultural, economic, political, and technological changes forecast for the coming century.

4\. a. Develop a comparative "shopping list" for the purchase of burial services. The list should include all items and services incorporated in the traditional funeral.

b. Visit at least three funeral firms and attempt to gather comparative cost data.

c. Prepare an analysis of the comparative data using descriptive statistics.

d. Explain the difference and similarities in the products and prices of the firms compared.

e. What decisions and recommendations result from your research?

Supplementary Readings

Books

Bernard, Hugh Y. *The Law of Death.* Dobbs Ferry, N.Y.: Oceana Publications, 1966.

Bowman, LeRoy. *The American Funeral.* Washington, D.C.: Public Affairs Press, 1959.

Brown, James A. *Approaches to the Social Dimensions of Mortuary Practices.* Washington, D.C.: Society for American Archaeology, 1971.

Dowd, Quincy L. *Funeral Management and Costs.* Chicago: University of Chicago Press, 1921.

Erhardt, Carl L. *Mortality and Morbidity in the United States.* Cambridge, Mass.: Harvard University Press, 1974.

Krieger, Wilbur M. *A Complete Guide to Funeral Service Management.* Englewood Cliffs, N.J.: Prentice-Hall, 1962.

Mitford, Jessica. *The American Way of Death.* New York: Simon & Schuster, 1963.

Raether, Howard C. *Successful Funeral Service Practice.* Englewood Cliffs, N.J.: Prentice-Hall, 1971.

Articles

"Burial Business Hears Voices." *Business Week,* November 14, 1960, p. 80.

"A Changing Way of Death." *Time,* April 11, 1960, p. 60.

"Cremations in the United States." *The NCBVA Bulletin,* April 1971, p. 2.

"The Funeral Industry: Some Harbingers of Change." *Consumer Reports* 30 (1965): 284.

Head, Ralph A. "The Reality of Death — What Happens When It is Ignored?" *Casket & Sunnyside* 101 (1971): 20.

Horn, Fred. "Cryonics: Challenge to the Funeral Industry." *Casket & Sunnyside* 90 (1969): 62.

Karpel, Craig. "Immortality is Fully Deductible." *Playboy,* October 1971, p. 250.

Wheatley, Edward W. "The Burial Industry 2071 — Sales to Marketing." *Casket & Sunnyside* 102 (1972): 65-67.

6
Women's Role in Business

"Professor Williams, call for you. Extension 53."
"Thanks, Barb. I'll take it in my office."
"Hello, Profession Williams? Hi, this is Rick Richards. How are you?"

It wasn't an unusual phone call. A former student, now a successful executive with a large newspaper chain, probably calling to reminisce. The small talk was interesting and enjoyable. It's always pleasing to learn that a bright collegiate prospect has performed so well in the professional ranks of business. After five minutes of catching up, Rick shifted to the real purpose of his call.

"We may have an outstanding opportunity for one of your students. Our circulation manager is retiring. We are converting the position to an executive training slot. Under this new arrangement, the candidate selected to fill the position will probably remain as circulation manager for approximately two years. During that time, the executive will have a great opportunity to learn our business and will likely be promoted to greater responsibility as the career pattern progresses. Do you have any outstanding candidates to recommend?"

"Well, Rick, how soon would you like to fill the vacancy?"

"We'll need to start someone within the next thirty to thirty-five days, and the person will have to be full time."

"Rick, that eliminates our graduating seniors. They wouldn't be able to help you until January. Wait a minute — how about a master's degree candidate? Would such a person be overqualified?"

"Heck, no! In fact, an MBA would be just great! But I didn't think anyone would be graduating from the current program until June."

"No, Rick. Actually we graduated about thirty people this August. There have been some program changes since you left."

"Come to think of it, professor, an MBA idea is probably what we should have been thinking about from the beginning. Let me outline the job description for you. I'll keep my fingers crossed that one of your best graduates may still be available."

Position: Manager — Circulation Division

Responsibilities: Maintain existing customer service with a primary objective of no subscription cancellations. Handle and resolve customer complaints. Administer new subscription processing. Develop and execute six-month marketing plans aimed at promoting the paper and increasing circulation. Administer delivery system. The primary responsibility of this executive is marketing, the secondary responsibility is administration. An office staff of approximately ten full-time persons will be under direct supervision of the manager.

Compensation: Starting salary, approximately $14,000 annually. Wide range of fringe benefits, including a $50 weekly car allowance, reitrement plan, hospitalization, insurance, two weeks paid vacation, plus all holidays. Regular salary reviews.

Qualifications: College graduate, business or journalism major preferred.

"Rick, our stars must all be in the correct positions. I've just the candidate for you — Phil Johnson. Phil holds a bachelor's degree in marketing, returned to our MBA program after two years as a sales representative for a package goods company. After less than one year on the job, Phil was promoted to sales manager. We have had nothing but glowing reports from Phil's undergraduate school and former employer. I would rank Phil in the top five percent of our MBAs. Are you interested?"

"Wow! You said it! Have Phil call me. By the way, professor, how old was Phil when the MBA was awarded?"

"Twenty-six."

"Perfect. We like to keep our executives entering the training program under age thirty. I'd like to see Phil within the next few days. Is that possible?"

"I'm sure that can be arranged. Thanks so much for sharing this opportunity with us Rick. I'm sure we've found the right person for you."

A Few Days Later

"Professor Williams, Rick Richards calling for you. Extension 53."

"Good morning, Rick. How's our favorite newspaper executive?"

"Fine, professor. Say, I want to thank you for sending Johnson down to us. Probably one of the most impressive graduates we've seen in a long time."

"Great, Rick. I'm glad it's working out."

"Well, it isn't exactly. Well, you see, we really weren't thinking of a woman for the executive program. Know what I mean?"

"Well, Rick, I'm not sure I do. How did Johnson react to your rejection?"

"Frankly, Professor, I didn't have the heart to be that blunt — know what I mean? I hope you understand my problem here. The other executives suggested that you could do a better job in breaking the news to Johnson than we could. I know I can count on you to do that for us . . . Professor, I've got a long distance call on another line. Have to run now."

"Okay, Rick, my intercom is buzzing too. Good-bye. Yes, Barb?"

"Professor Williams, Phyllis Johnson is here to see you."

"Send her in."

Why was Phyllis Rejected?

The preceding account is adapted from a real world situation. Professor Williams didn't accept Ms. Johnson's rejection without further investigation. When pressed, the business firm in question attempted to defend their rejection of an otherwise qualified and proven job candidate on the basis of her sex. "The job would sometimes involve long hours"; "she would have to associate with ['supervise'] a lot of men"; "we don't feel women should be placed in that type of job"; "she might get married;" "she might get pregnant." After it became clear that none of these reasons seemed to satisfy Professor Williams, the employer thought for a while and came up with the clincher — "Sometimes the manager might have to lift bundled papers. Those bundles weigh thirty-five to forty pounds. You can see that this would be no job for a woman." There was a long silence in the conversation when Professor Williams commented that his wife lifts and totes his 45-pound son and 35-pound daughter a total of perhaps fifty times a day. But no matter, Phyllis wanted the job, but didn't have a 1,000-to-1 chance of getting it.

Discrimination in Business

In the following pages, you will be asked to consider several aspects of one form of discrimination practiced by business. But before we focus on discrimination against women by the business sector, we need to gain a broader perspective.

Discrimination may be defined as the act of showing favoritism toward individuals or groups at the expense of other individuals or groups. Discriminatory behavior, defined in the negative sense, is not based on reason or the full facts, but rather on suspicion stemming from cultural value judgments. These cultural values are deeply held, are learned early in life, and are difficult to modify. We call a person who discriminates in this manner "prejudiced." A prejudiced person "pre-judges" others, usually by abstracting one or two characteristics and generalizing them into a stereotype without bothering to collect more evidence prior to passing judgment. Like all values, the values operative in prejudicial behavior undergo evolutionary change. These changes reflect, usually with some lag, the environmental changes and mutating objectives of a society. To force a woman to relinquish her family role, leave the home, and take a job with a business firm would have been prejudicial behavior 100 years ago. To force a woman to stay at home and not take the same job is prejudicial today.

Before you condemn business as a major social villian ask yourself honestly if prejudicial practices and behavior are not also evident in your government, church, educational system, military, social organizations, family, and yourself. Is business the major causal factor of discrimination, or is it merely reflective of our society's values?

Vive la Différence

Of course men and women are different and isn't it great! Also, each man and each woman is different, one from the other. But does the difference in female/male physiology mean that sex should be used as the basis for the assignment of life's roles? Many people think so. The belief that women have certain natural roles to play in society's plan serves as the primary basis for sex discrimination. The assumption is that God ordained the sexual roles and that they are, and forever will be, "right."

The so-called natural or instinctive argument against changing women's roles is based on the historical precedents ascribed to females in the animal kingdom since the early days of the recorded history of man. The female feathers the nest, gives birth, nurtures the young, and is responsible for the home. The male leaves home each morning to hunt, kill, and provide for his family, returning the the security of home after the day's work is performed. The female does not "work" — she stays at home. The assumption made by those utilizing the "instinctive role" argument is that the social environment is an immutable constant.

> Whenever people move to change their social environment, the defenders of tradition rise to the occasion by proclaiming the natural or "instinctive" basis for patterns. They do this by skillful use of anthropological material or by means of animal or human performance in the past or present which takes no account of the material or cultural bases for sex differences. Although biological differences have often been associated with differences in social opportunity or social power, this does not prove that differences in social opportunity or social power between men and women are themselves innate or immutable.[1]

The skillful use of anthropological material referred to in the preceding quotation consists of selective analogies between women of the American frontier, selected primitive societies, and certain animal species. Anyone wishing to counter the "instinctive" argument can find examples that offset those depicting the "traditional" role of women.[2] What is important

[1]Carol Andreas, *Sex and Caste in America* (Englewood Cliffs, N.J.: Prentice-Hall, Inc., 1971), p. 7.

[2]Andreas. See Chapter 1 for detailed counterarguments to the "instinctive" or "naturalistic" view.

here is that the total social environment *is* changing. As society, its institutions, and its values change, the roles of individuals are transformed. Today women might interpret "vive la différence" as a proclamation of opportunity for feminine role modification. Whatever the specific circumstances surrounding each individual case, the primary basis for prejudicial attitudes toward women is "naturalism." The primary argument against naturalism is that society no longer depends wholly on force, physical strength, and superior size to accomplish its objectives and fulfill its needs. The time required for completion of the homemaking tasks assigned to women has been reduced through technology. Women therefore have a right to reject the historical definition of their roles and work toward role redefinition more congruent with modern times.

Women's Place

Should women be permitted to work outside the home and family? The question has little meaning. Women have worked outside the home and continue to do so in ever-increasing numbers, as indicated by table 1.[3]

Table 1
Women in the Civilian Labor Force
Selected Years, 1900-1970*

Year	Number (in thousands)	As Percent of All Workers	As percent of female Population
1900	4,999	18.1	20.0
1920	8,229	20.4	22.7
1930	10,396	21.9	23.6
1940	13,783	25.4	28.6
1945	19,290	36.1	38.1
1947	16,664	27.9	30.8
1950	18,389	29.6	33.9
1955	20,548	31.6	35.7
1960	23,240	33.4	37.7
1965	26,200	35.2	39.2
1970	31,520	38.1	43.3

*Sixteen years of age and over — pre-1940 figures include 14 years of age or older.

If, as it appears in table 1, woman's place is not only in the home but also

[3]Francine Blau Weisskoff, "Women's Place in the Labor Market," *American Economic Review* (May 1973), p. 16s. Note: data developed from: U.S. Dept. of Labor, Women's Bureau, 1969, *Handbook on Women Workers*, p. 10. U.S. Dept. of Labor, Manpower Administration, *Manpower Report of the President*, Washington, D.C., 1971, pp. 203-250.

as an important component of the work force, why have businesses and other major employers been singled out as chronic discriminators against women? Table 2 provides a revealing answer.[4]

Table 2.
Occupations in Which 70 Per Cent or More
of the Workers Were Women, 1960

Occupation	Per cent female	Per cent of female labor force in Occupation
Attendants in physicians' and dentists' offices	98	0.3
Chambermaids and maids	98	0.8
Nurses	98	2.8
Receptionists	98	0.6
Dressmakers and seamstresses	97	0.5
Private houshold workers	96	7.9
Stenographers, typists, and secretaries	96	10.0
Telephone operators	96	1.6
Sewers and stitchers	94	2.6
Dieticians and nutritionists	93	0.1
Demonstrators	92	0.1
Milliners	92	0.0
Hairdressers and cosmetologists	89	1.2
Boarding and lodging housekeepers	88	0.1
File clerks	86	0.5
Librarians	86	0.3
Waitresses, counter and fountain workers	84	4.0
Hospital attendants, practical nurses, and midwives	81	2.3
Housekeepers and stewards	80	0.6
Textile spinners	79	0.2
Knitting mill operatives	78	0.2
Dancers and dancing teachers	77	0.1
Library attendants and assistants	77	0.1
Apparel and accessories operatives	74	1.3
Office machine operators	74	1.1
Laundry and dry cleaning operatives	72	1.3
Teachers	72	5.4
Fruit, nut, and vegetable graders and packers	71	0.1
Attendants, professional and personal services	70	0.2
Total		51.5

[4] Valerie Oppenheimer, "The Sex-Labelling of Jobs," *Industrial Relations* VII (May 1968), p. 220.

Note the high percentage of females in the relatively lower level business related jobs, i.e., receptionists, secretaries, operators, file clerks, cashiers, office machine operators, etc. Note also the occupations employing the higher percentages of the female labor force. This is only one small bit of the massive array of data that support the charge that women work, in the main, in positions of lower authority, responsibility, status, pay, and benefits.

Related to the types of work performed by women is the issue of prejudicial compensation. There are two basic sub-issues involved: first, women are not paid enough for the work they do; second, women are paid less than men when there is no difference in work performed. Table 3 illustrates the point.[5]

Table 3

Median Earnings of Full-time Year-round Workers, by Sex and Occupational Group, 1968

Major Occupational Group	Median Wage or Salary Income Women	Men	Women's median wage or salary income as percent of men's
Professional and Technical Workers	$6,691	$10,151	65.9
Non-farm managers, Officials, and Proprietors	5,635	10,340	54.5
Clerical Workers	4,789	7,351	65.1
Sales Workers	3,461	8,549	40.5
Operatives	3,991	6,738	59.2
Service Workers (except private household)	3,332	6,058	55.0

Please note that while the data imply vast differences between the compensation of men and women, it is assumed that the actual work performed in each category is differentiated only by sex. Such an assumption is undoubtedly invalid in many cases.

The analysis of starting salary offers for bachelor's degree candidates in tables 4 and 5 provides an interesting insight concerning the types of positions offered and starting salary differentials in similar fields.[6]

[5]U.S. Department of Commerce, Bureau of the Census, *Current Population Report* No. 66, p. 60.

[6]Richard B. Mancke, "Lower Pay for Women: A Case of Economic Discrimination?" *Industrial Relations* (Oct. 1971), pp. 324-325.

Table 4

National Average Monthly Salary Offers by Positions
for Women Bachelor Degree Candidates

Position	No. of Offers 1969-1970	Average $ Offer, 1969-70
Accountant	241	$820
Airline Stewardess	20	462
Business Trainee	362	611
Community and Service Organization Worker	193	569
EDP Programmer	299	752
Engineer	38	857
Home Economist	38	556
Library Interne	25	474
Mathematician/Statistician	116	740
Medical Worker	112	623
Merchandising Trainee	194	559
Research Assistant — nonscientific	75	608
Research Assistant — scientific	111	637
Secretary/Receptionist	141	478
Writer	92	518
Other	108	615
Total	2,165	$642

Table 5

National Average Monthly Salary Offers by Curiculum
For Men Bachelor's Degree Candidates

Curriculum	No. of Offers 1969-1970	Average $ Offers 1969-1970
Accounting	3,275	$836
Business — general	3,027	721
Humanities and Social Science	897	700
Marketing and Distribution	818	702
Engineering — Aeronautical	624	850
Engineering — Chemical	2,372	902
Engineering — Civil	1,715	837
Engineering — Electrical	4,854	869
Engineering — Industrial	1,137	849
Engineering — Mechanical	4,428	867
Engineering — Metallurgical	378	873
Chemistry	251	825
Physics	152	827
Mathematics	469	794
Total	24,396	$832

The macro statistics clearly indicate that while women are an important segment of society's work force, they have far to go in achieving parity with men relative to the range of career opportunity, level achievement within career fields, and compensation.

Stereotypes — The Language of Discrimination

Culturally, society maintains a sex-dichotomy. Since people are primarily defined by their sex, not as persons, managers or other non-sexual categories, sex linked expectations of behavior and relationships have evolved. As "we all know," men are tough, dominant, active leaders, — rational; women are tender, submissive, passive, followers, — emotional. Defined from such assumptions, most jobs have become sex-typed.[7]

Sex typing, along with racial and religious typing, is one of the prevalent ways in which society conveniently classifies minority members. Sex typing is a form of stereotyping. Stereotyping is a powerful mental process that results in automatic value judgments about large sets or subsets of people or issues without the necessity of gathering and evaluating evidence. Stereotyping is a popular form of human mental nonprocess because it offers a simple problem resolution. The circuitry of the brain is jumped as the stereotyper reacts to a stimulus with a programmed response. Stereotyping is like a conditioned reflex based upon reinforced learning. The stereotypes employed are often learned from family peers, are based on and influence values, and gradually develop into beliefs. Beliefs based on conditioned stereotype learning may become absolute, equated with Aristotle's level of "certainty" discussed in chapter two.

Stereotypes and Sex Typing — Characteristics and Examples

Stereotypes function as screens that block out other experiences or information which would lead to personalized responses. Stereotypic screens filter responses to women and provide certain consistent patterns of thinking and reacting. . . .[8] The power of sterotypic expectation of women and the images they conjure up are all encompassing indeed.[9]

Let's examine some characteristics of stereotypic filters and their application in discrimination against women in business.

1. Stereotypes are resistant to change: "Women have always been the weaker sex — how can they be expected to stand up under the pressures of business?"

2. Stereotypes are deep-rooted in collective history, perpetuated by

---

[7]Rosalind Loring and Theodore Wells, *Breakthrough: Women Into Management* (New York: Van Nostrand Reinhold, 1972), p. 131.

[8]Loring and Wells, p. 131.   [9]Loring and Wells, p. 133.

legend and religious folklore: "Women have been the pillar of the home. This has been true for centuries. Woman's place is in the home, not in the executive conference rooms of business."

3. Stereotypes are not responsive to evidence: "OK, Mary did solve our dealer problem in the Southwest Region, but she just got lucky. You know — women's intuition."

4. What applies to one person in a stereotyped group applies to all persons in the group: Joan responds sharply to a sex loaded remark at the office. "Well, what do you expect? Women are too emotional."

5. What applies to the stereotyped group also applies to each member. "Women are too emotional. How else did you expect Joan to react? After all, she's a woman."

6. Each group member is exactly like the other: "Of course Joan overreacted. So would Jean, Sara, and Diane. After all, they're all women."

7. Stereotypes don't transfer to nongroup members: "Boy, Bill in accounting really got mad this morning." No stereotyping, i.e., no one concludes that because Bill got angry, "men are too emotional."

8. Stereotypes measure with undefined yardsticks: "Women are too sensitive." The use of the stereotyped conclusion does not specify any detailed comparative or contextual basis."

9. Comparative stereotypic judgments connote negative values: "Florence is too aggressive." Translation? Aggressive behavior in businessmen has a positive value. Aggressive behavior in women in business has a negative value.

10. Accepting and using stereotypes is one passport to group acceptance: JoAnn bristles and briskly leaves the room when unjustly reprimanded in front of her coworkers. The office manager shrugs, turns to JoAnne's male subordinates, and asks, "Isn't that just like a woman?"

11. Sex stereotypes elicit sex role behavior: The corporate executive committee meets to consider a plant emergency. The company president speaks: "Donna [Donna Billings, Corporate Vice President for Consumer Affairs], why don't you take the minutes?"

12. Only someone far above the stereotyped norm can escape stereotypic judgment: "Barbara is so far superior, we simply must promote her into the executive ranks." Translation? "Barbara's job performance has been far above the typical female performance and even better than the men in her division. We really can't find any basis on which to deny her an advancement."

13. Deviators from the stereotypic patterns are freaks, exceptions which prove the rule: "I must admit that Sandra is a capable manager. But when

they made her, they threw away the mold. She's a rare exception to the typical woman in business."[10]

As you come across instances of prejudicial behavior, listen and look for examples of stereotyped response. Extract the stereotypic language from the conversation or writing. Attempt to classify the basis for the stereotype from the preceding list. Use the example given within each classification chosen to "play back" the stereotype judgment to the individual evoking the stereotyped response. Keep probing — you'll have some fun and may be convinced of the shallow thinking and lack of rational analysis behind the stereotype. For example, if someone says "Florence is too aggressive," a negative value stereotype (number 9 in the preceding list), you might play back: "Is being aggressive in business bad?" "Why?" "In what context?"

We all engage in stereotyping. Stereotyping is a common, simple, and sometimes constructive variant of the generalization. Like the generalization, however, stereotyping should not be used or accepted as a substitute for evidential analysis of each situation on its own merits. Stereotyping is the major obstacle to situational analysis in issues involving prejudicial discriminatory behavior. Activation of your "stereotype early warning system" will facilitate identification and analysis of your own prejudices and those of others.

Women in Management — Objections and Responses

"Women in business? We need good secretaries and clerical help. Women are also excellent production workers in certain limited situations where the work is clean and not too strenuous."

"Give women equal consideration for all types of jobs, equal pay and access to executive positions? Of course we want to do that wherever we can, but as you are well aware, women present us with some special problems."

What are the "special problems" that prevent deserving and desirous female career candidates from obtaining more responsible and higher paying positions? Loring and Wells identify several major barriers to upwardly mobile females in business. Within each of the barrier areas, several specific objections are raised. The authors respond to these objections in an attempt to debunk the typical corporate rationale.[11]

1. Can women make a business career commitment?

O: (Objection) Women get married, quit work, or change jobs because of their husbands. Doesn't business have a right to know a woman's

[10]Loring and Wells, adapted from pp. 132-133.
[11]Loring and Wells. See pp. 146-162 for the complete analysis from which these materials are adapted.

personal plans for marriage, family, and how long they plan to remain on the job?

R: (Response) Yes, as long as men are also required to furnish the same information.

O: Women managers can become pregnant, quit, and waste the company's investment in training.

R: The majority of women have their last child by age 26, far before they would be considered for management positions. Once in management, women are less likely to leave than men. Better birth control for both sexes will minimize unplanned pregnancies and day-care facilities, both public and private, continue to increase in number.

O: When children are sick, women flee from the office.

R: Job absences for family illness and other emergencies occur with both men and women. Lower level female employees cannot justify the economics of staying on the job and paying the costs of qualified home care.

O: Women employees have a higher turnover rate than men.

R: U.S. Department of Labor statistics do not support this common objection. Job skill level, age, past record, and length of service are key correlates to turnover rates. "The frequency with which men leave for better jobs effectively offsets women leaving to have children."[12]

O: Women miss too much work due to absence.

R: Based on U.S. Department of Labor data, absentee rates are related to job level and are similar for both sexes.

O: Women don't want management positions. They will refuse promotion because their job will interfere with their personal lives.

R: Some women, as well as some men, will refuse higher positions. At issue here is providing equal opportunity for qualified women to be considered for and offered managerial positions.

O: Women don't need to work. They have men to take care of them. A man needs the job and income to satisfy his obligations as the breadwinner.

R: Department of Labor data reveal that only 59% of working women who are married have husbands present. Many women also have economic needs and motivations. In addition, commitment to a business career is often based on satisfying other needs and drives. Women, too, have noneconomic needs which result in career commitment.

2. *Physiological and Emotional Barriers*

O: Women's hormones cause a monthly problem. And menopause can upset women for months or years. How can they be expected to bring stability to responsible positions?

---

[12]Loring and Wells, p. 148.

R: Why penalize a woman for menses? Should a male executive be removed from responsibility because he has an ulcer? There is little evidence which supports this "incapacitating theory" of the menstrual cycle. The authors cite an endocrinology text that reports that approximately 50% of women have no symptoms of menopause and 45% continue to work without interruption. Only 5% were reported being incapacitated at intervals. Citing other authorities, the authors point out that male executives may also experience hormonal changes between ages 55 and 65. These changes are symptomized by tension, emotional instability, irritability, moodiness, memory lapses, and loss of concentration. There is also some evidence that all men experience monthly cyclical changes in hormonal balance.

O: Women overpersonalize criticism; they are not objective enough to accept the criticism inherent in the manager's responsible role.

R: Women typically have longer work experience in the same jobs as men. They are conditioned to objectivity and critical review. They learn to depersonalize criticism for the same reasons as men, i.e., their survival and progress.

O: Women don't control their emotions as well as men. What does a businessman do when a woman executive cries?

R: Business women in tears are usually entry level, young nonmanagers. By the time a woman becomes a executive, she learns how to cope in other ways with frustration and anger. She has to or she won't survive. Men may feel superior because they never display "weakness." More often, emotions are channeled into anger — a socially acceptable reaction for a man in business but not a woman.

The male values of stoic control have provided standards of appropriate behavior in the work world. What a relief it would be to both men and women if human feelings were permitted freer expression. It might reduce the ulcer and heart attack rates.[13]

O: Women are too soft. They don't have the mental toughness necessary for making hard business decisions. They don't have the staying power for the long and difficult negotiations common to the executive calling.

R: True professional maturity is a rare asset in both men and women. Women too can be skillful strategists and negotiators. They have the patience and "cool" to pursue long-range objectives.

3.*The Distractive Shadow of the Sexual Relationship*

O: When women are required to manage men, sexual undercurrents, tensions, fantasies, and actual encounters may disrupt the business.

R: Women in business repress sexuality if it occurs. They want their success to be based on job competence, not sex. Men don't seem to worry

[13]Loring and Wells, p. 153.

about the business falling apart because of potential sexual attraction between executives, employees, and their attractive female secretaries. The woman or man being overcome by passion and surrendering to the sexual urge is a myth perpetrated by advertising and the movies. In the past, where sexual relationships between male managers and female employees distracted from business performance, the female was often terminated. The male was "counseled." Such double standards may no longer be upheld. Recent EEOC rulings indicate termination of the female in such a case constitutes sex bias.

O: Women will use sex to get what they want.

R: Certainly sexual coercion is an advancement technique practiced to some degree by women, as well as men, in business. Male executives may use call girls and cooperative secretaries to entertain certain important clients. Few women executives, however, are foolish enough to risk their hard-earned status and incomes on a bet that sex will have more long-term value to business than job productivity.

4. *The Masculine Social Setting of Business*

O: Women are unwilling to give up their special status. They would rather be protected than be equal in the tough competition for status and money.

R: The 42% of working women who are unmarried or separated are already independent to a large degree. How can business equate the drudgery of housework and lowly office work with "special status" or "protection"? Women must be free to determine whether they prefer to pursue the pedestal or the corporate presidency.

O: Women managers will expect the courtesies due their sex. This may be incongruous in the business setting.

R: Manners, courtesy, and consideration between both sexes are not incompatible with organizational rank.

O: Businessmen may sometimes relieve tension with profanity and off-color jokes.

R: In today's society, women are exposed to uncensored language in a wide variety of contexts. The roughness of the company warehouse is greatly modified at the executive level. Women are already exposed to most of the world faced by men. Assuming that their "shell-like" ears will disintegrate from office language is naive.

O: The business setting often includes social drinking.

R: Male and female executives should be held accountable for their drinking behavior.

O: Customers, other male executives, and male employees will be ill at ease when a woman picks up the check for lunch or drinks.

R: Where women executives have expense accounts, men soon get used to a female paying a bill. Where a man is very sensitive about paying, let him pay. He is probably on an expense account too.

5. *The Feminity/Masculinity Paradox*
O: Women in management positions will soon lose their femininity.

R: If femininity is a natural difference between the sexes, it will not be lost any more than a man would lose his masculinity.

O: As a woman progresses in her management career, she will become too masculine.

R: Women who are interested in management come with various styles, as do men. Strange that men first worry about women managers acting too feminine and then suspect that they will become too masculine (meaning aggressive?). To paraphrase Freud, "What *do* men want? My God, what do they want?"[14]

What Do Men Want?

I've asked several women in business what they believe businessmen expect from them. This totally nonscientific "unsurvey" produced three basic classifications of response:

1. Businessmen expect women in the office to be surrogate mothers, wives, daughters, and, occasionally, lovers. Women are part of the decor. They are expected to be attractive, prompt, dependable, uncomplaining, and anxious to please. The relationship is one of total domination by the male. Speak when spoken to if that's the boss' mood. Flatter and sympathize when the boss is depressed. Quietly untangle the snarls he causes and let him take the credit. Express one's own feelings or bring personal problems to the office and you've had it!

2. Poor men! Women's liberation has made them a little crazy. There are several interesting reactions. A few businessmen mouth the slogans of the libbers attempting to "snow" us. But as for instituting any changes, it's business as usual. Some men managers sincerely sympathize with women seeking change, but they seem frustrated in defining what they can do personally. Other businessmen take action too quickly. Promoting underqualified women to management positions believing they have taken positive steps, their conscience is clear. In such cases, the unprepared female executive may botch the job, "proving" the old stereotypes and reinforcing the prejudices held by the majority of management.

3. Blindly blaming businessmen or other organizations for discrimination against women is naive. Our whole society sex types individuals and prescribes their roles. Actually, our large organizations — business, government, education, etc. — are now becoming aware of the need for change and have begun to react positively by hiring, training, and promot-

[14]Loring and Wells, p. 154.

ing qualified women into management ranks. Like any basic social change, equality for women will take decades. Prejudice of any kind will never be totally erased. But business is now doing its share to change things. "I'm proud to be a businesswoman."

The Law — New Ally for Women in Business?

Our democratic ideal of equal protection under the law has historically been implemented by "protecting" women, i.e., preventing women from determining their own roles.

> The United States Supreme Court (in *Bradwell v. Illinois*, 1872) upheld a state barring women from the practice of law, stating:
> "Man is, or should be, woman's protector and defender. The natural and proper timidity and delicacy which belongs to the female sex evidently unfits it for many of the occupations of civil life."[15]

The duty of the law to "protect" women is illustrated by a U.S. Supreme Court pronouncement in 1908: "... history discloses the fact that woman has always been dependent upon man ... looking at it from the viewpoint of the effort to maintain an independent position in life, she is not upon a equality ... she is properly placed in a class by herself."[16]

In a 1948 case, a woman was disqualified from a bartender's job. The law offered her no remedy as the Supreme Court ruled that her case would have merit only if she were the wife or daughter of the male owner. Equally illustrative of our highest court's sex role typing is an excerpt from the explanation of the ruling:

> The fact that women may now have achieved the virtues that men have long claimed as their prerogatives and now indulge in vices that men have long practiced, does not preclude the States from drawing a sharp line between the sexes, certainly in such matters as the regulation of liquor traffic. The Constitution does not require legislatures to reflect sociological insight, or shifting social standards, any more than it requires them to keep abreast of the latest scientific standards.[17]

Two major legal developments hold promise for giving women in business and other careers equality under the law. Title VII of the Civil Rights Act of 1964 prohibits discrimination for reasons of sex in hiring, promotion, and firing. The law applies to all employers of 25 or more employees and includes labor unions and employment agencies. The Equal Pay Act of 1965 prohibits sex-based discriminatory compensation practices. The Equal Employment Opportunity Commission is the major federal agency charged with administering complaints filed under these antidiscrimination acts.

[15]Diane Schulder, "Women and the Law," *Atlantic Monthly*, March, 1970, p. 103.
[16]Schulder, p. 103.   [17]Schulder, p. 103.

An employee who believes he or she has been the object of discrimination must file a complaint with EEOC. A staff member then investigates and submits a report to the commissioners, who decide on the merits. Then the staff must bargain with the employer or union on an acceptable remedy. If there's an impasse, the complaint must then file a suit in court, since EEOC is not entitled to take legal action against employers.[18]

There is, of course, a great gap in time between the passage of remedial legislation in any field and substantial reduction in the injustices the law seeks to prevent. Massive federal legislation may have the net short-term effect of only signaling intent. States, counties, cities, and individual citizens all operate based on their own laws, ordinances, and value codes. Even under the consensus of unanimous social pressure, few laws totally solve the problems that caused their passage. Murder, kidnapping, and armed robbery all carry serious consequences for the convicted offender, but, we still murder, kidnap, and rob at gunpoint. Individuals expecting instant social change based on legislation have been sobered by the ponderous pace of the EEOC.

By 1971, seven years after the passage of the Civil Rights Act, the EEOC faced a backlog of 26,000 unsettled discrimination cases. The total continues to mount. Over a third of the discrimination complaints involve sex discrimination. In the area of sex bias in hiring, complaints by women exceed those by men four to one.[19] There is continued dispute concerning the EEOC's efficacy and the definition of its power. Some congressmen feel the EEOC should be given greater regulatory and enforcement power. A strong EEOC could cut the backlog and settle complaints quickly. Supporters of a strong EEOC cite evidence that the National Labor Relations Board settles more than 95% of the cases brought before it without referring cases to the courts. Opponents argue that a federal court would give the alleged discriminator a fairer hearing. Reacting to the "fairer hearing in court" argument, one editor states:

> The argument carries little weight. Courts are overburdened with present juridictions; dumping another 26,000 or more cases into legal channels will only serve to clog them. A recent survey shows the median interval for a nonjury trial in US district courts is 17 months. That's how long it takes once you've convinced the government to take your case, hired your own attorney, filed and won the right to be heard.[20]

The ERA — A Final Answer?

The proposed Equal Rights Amendment to the Constitution of the

---

[18]"Toothless Tiger," *The New Republic*, February 26, 1972, p. 8.

[19]Alice S. Rossi, "Job Discrimination and What Women Can Do About It," *Atlantic Monthly*, March 1970, p. 101.

[20]"Equal Opportunities," *The New Republic*, October 30, 1971, p. 10.

United States could serve as the foundation stone for major long-term modification in the role of women. The proposed 27th Amendment reads:

Section 1. Equality of rights under the law shall not be denied or abridged by the United States or by any State on account of sex.
Section 2. The Congress shall have the power to enforce, by appropriate legislation, the provisions of this article.
Section 3. This amendment shall take effect two years after the date of ratification.

Constitutional amendments require an affirmative two-thirds vote (38 states in favor) for adoption. Mrs. Anne Armstrong, counselor to Richard Nixon and the only woman in the former Nixon Cabinet, predicted adoption of the ERA in the 1970s.

We got ratification by 30 states in the first year after it cleared Congress, and we need only eight more states to put it over... I've stood ready to cooperate. And the President did reiterate in two of his state of the union messages his continuing support of the ERA.[21]

ERA supporters cite the need for supervision of various individual discriminatory laws and practices a Constitutional amendment would provide. In effect, all laws and practices resulting in sex discrimination would be rendered unconstitutional.

Two of the more quotable quotes made by congressmen opposed to ERA include:[22]

This would absolutely destroy the law which makes it the duty of the husband to support the wife and children... It would destroy alimony laws and child-custody laws... If we need any new amendment, it would be to ban Congress from passing any legislation in election years. (Senator Sam Ervin, North Carolina)

...This [is a] blunderbuss amendment... There is no equality except in a cemetery. There are differences in physical structure and biological function ...There is more difference between a male and female than between a horse chestnut and a chestnut horse. (Representative Emanuel Celler, New York)

Predictions concerning the effects of the ERA on the employment of women, women in general, and American society seem to cover all possibilities. "Disastrous" effects of the ERA cited by opponents are characterized in the following quote.

Their scenario for the ERA-era is a world of "unisex" restrooms, legalized homosexual marriages, and military combat duty for mothers of small children; they envision a nation in which rape and prostitution are no longer criminal offenses, in which there are no maternity leaves for working

[21]"Progress in Role of Women is Steady and it is Sure," *U. S. News and World Report,* May 14, 1973, p. 68.
[22]Robert Sherril, "That Equal Rights Amendment— What, Exactly Does It Mean?" *The New York Times Magazine,* September 20, 1970, p. 26.

mothers, no child support laws to protect divorcees and their children. And lesser fears, one anti-liberation speaker predicts that the amendment will do away with all-male and all-female groups, like Rotary International and the Daughters of the American Revolution.[23]

ERA supporters present a totally different picture. In addition to establishing a final legal basis to end discrimination in employment, the ERA's potential positive benefits are alleged to include:

1. Equal age and benefits under Social Security and other pension plans.

2. "Protective" legislation restricting opportunity for women employees would be ended.

3. Women's property, contractual, and credit rights (and obligations) would be equal with men's.

4. Equality would be brought into laws relating to married women.

5. Criminal penalties would be equal between sexes.

6. The legal age of majority would be equalized.

7. Sex discrimination in state-supported schools would be ended.

8. Women would not be forced to assume their husband's name at marriage.

9. Alimony and child custody would not be based on stereotyped sex roles.

In response to charges that ERA will create a unisex world, supporters stress:

> ...that legislation is permissible which deals with a physical characteristic unique to one sex. Thus, for example, legislation allowing maternity benefits would not be affected, since no matter how the law is rewritten in sexually neutral terms, it can still apply only to women. Likewise, laws that deal with rape and prostitution will still be valid. Prostitution laws would, however, have to be extended to apply to male prostitutes. It is possible also that the amendment might be interpreted to make buyer as well as seller — that is, male patron as well as female prostitutes — subject to prostitution laws.
>
> The unfounded charge that separate restrooms for men and women will be eliminated by the ERA must also be laid to rest. To begin with, a society's body of laws is firmly grounded in its mores and folkways, in the collective moral attitudes of its members. It is absurd to believe that courts or legislative bodies will act to establish as law a practice contrary to common sense and the commonly accepted standards of propriety. Moreover, the principle of the "right to privacy" already recognized by the courts in other connections, applies as well to the separation of the sexes for activities involving disrobing, sleeping and personal bodily functions.[24]

---

[23]"I Didn't Raise My Girl to be a Soldier: Sense and Nonsense About the ERA," *The Christian Century,* October 25, 1972, p. 1056.

[24]"I Didn't Raise My Girl to be a Solider," pp. 1057-1058.

Women at Work in Other Cultures

Early in this chapter, it was suggested that as the social environment changes, the previously held individual roles also change. Supporting this idea is the rather rapid change in women's roles in the Soviet Union.

Soviet education for women has resulted in striking differences in the numbers of women white-collar workers and professionals compared to the United States. About 50% of the Soviet white-collar labor force are women. About half of this group have had specialized education. Women comprise a majority of the semiprofessional and professional Soviet labor force. In the U.S., women physicians comprise less than 10% of the profession. Approximately 75% of Soviet physicians are women. About one-third of Soviet engineers are women. That figure for the United States is about 1%. About the only area where Soviet women hold fewer positions than U.S. is *women in politics*.

Is Business Really Serious About Women?

This is a difficult question to answer conclusively. My own estimate of the situation is that business is now becoming aware of its bias against women. As this awareness spreads, assisted by the law, firms will move "affirmatively" to provide opportunity for women. Women will make a positive contribution to the firm and pave the way for faster and broader acceptance of those who follow. How long will this take? What is your guess?

The New York City Commission on Human Rights, in hearings keynoted by Dr. Margaret Mead, pursued the topic of women in private industry. Several business firms were invited to testify concerning their policies and progress in attacking the problem of sex discrimination. Five companies accepted the commission's invitation. They were the New York Times, Bankers Trust Company, Bell Telephone Company, J. Walter Thompson Company, and Merrill, Lynch, Pierce, Fenner & Smith. You are encouraged to read the testimony and responses to questioning contained in the hearing transcript. The testimony of the public is also interesting and relevant.[25] As a result of the hearings, the commission developed specific recommendations in the following areas: employment, professions, government, New York State labor law, pregnancy and fringe benefits, household workers, taxation, social services, housing and credit practices, education, law, and politics.[26] The recommendations concerning

---

[25]*Women's Role in Contemporary Society: The Report of the New York City Commission on Human Rights* (New York: Avon Books, 1972), pp. 180-340.

[26]*Women's Role in Contemporary Society.* See pp. 29-45.

"Equal Opportunity in Business and Industry" are summarized below.

The Commission recommends an affirmative action program by business and industry with special focus on the following areas:

1. Institution of a "skills and interest" inventory file of female employees as a primary source for filling promotion and transfer vacancies and for selection for management training programs.

2. Affirmative programs for women, including recruitment at women's and coeducational institutions, use of female recruiters, development of female referral sources, revision of advertising of female referral sources, and revision of advertising policies to encourage female applicants.

3. Institution of an "affirmative action file" of female applicants as a primary reference for filling vacancies for which there are no presently qualified female employees.

4. Review of employment application and interview procedures to eliminate nonjob-related questions bearing on marital status, family planning, etc.

5. Annual review of selection criteria and procedures to ensure that women are receiving equal consideration for all job levels and all training programs.

6. Elimination of job classifications limited to one sex, of different titles for jobs requiring the same skills and/or duties, and elimination of discriminatory seniority systems.

7. Annual review of wages and salaries in relation to duties and performance in order to ensure equal pay for equal work.

8. Institution of management training and tuition refund programs for upgrading of clerical and secretarial personnel to paraprofessional and professional status.

9. Institution of programs of part-time work, as well as of flexible and staggered work hours, with part-time workers entitled to proportional employment benefits and promotions.

10. Establishment of industrially sponsored day-care centers — open 24 hours when necessary — with policy and supervision decided in cooperation with the employees whose children are enrolled.

11. Reexamination of retirement, life insurance, disability, and health plans to eliminate features discriminatory toward women.

12. Revision of pregnancy leave policies to eliminate arbitrary time of mandatory leave, to provide for use of sick leave for pregnancy and related conditions, and to provide for job security and continuation of seniority and other employment benefits.

The Commission also recommends:

1. Legislation giving full enforcement powers to the Equal Employment Opportunity Commission.

2. Vigorous use of the compliance review procedures and contract suspension power of the Office of Federal Contract Compliance in cases of sex discrimination.

3. Amendment of the State and City Human Rights Laws to make it a lawful and nondiscriminatory practice for an employer voluntarily to plan for and increase the employment of women.

4. Budgetary allocations by federal, state, and city governments and by private industry for industrial- and community-sponsored training courses for housewives who are now ready to enter or reenter the labor force on either a part- or full-time basis.

5. Use of the licensing power of the New York City Department of Consumer Affairs to suspend or revoke licenses of employment agencies found practicing discrimination.

6. Determination by federal, state, and city regulatory agencies that unlawful discrimination is a ground for denial or suspension of licenses, rate increases, and other privileges within the granting jurisdiction of these agencies.

7. Appointment of women in increasing numbers to the boards of directors and to high executive positions in business and industry.

Discussion Questions

1. Assume you are Phyllis Johnson.
   a. How would you have reacted to the job rejection discussed early in the chapter?
   b. Would you have taken any further action? Why or why not?
   c. If you decided to pursue the matter further, exactly what would you do?

2. a. In your opinion is the cause of prejudicial behavior rooted in our business system?
   b. If so, in what ways is prejudice evidenced in the business setting?
   c. If not, where does prejudice originate, how is it reinforced, and what is the role of business in its perpetuation?
   d. "If it really wanted to, business could put an end to prejudice."
   How do you react to this statement?
   What constraints does business face in fighting prejudice?
   In what areas can business help reduce prejudice?

4. How do you feel the following institutions compare with business relative to prejudicial behavior?
   a. (1) the church, (2) government, (3) education, (4) social clubs, (5) the scientific community, and (6) the artistic community.
   b. What reasons can you suggest for any differences or similarities you have noted?

5. If you had the opportunity to hire an equally qualified woman or a man for a middle management position which would you hire? On what basis would you make your decision?

6. Analyze the statistical data presented in tables 2 through 6. What conclusions do you reach?

7. Assume that you move into a new neighborhood/school/job considerably different in location and social economic status from your previous locale.

    a. How might the new area residents/students/employees stereotype you? Specifically, what terms might they use?

    b. How might you use stereotyping to describe your new environment?

8. "Stereotyping is merely a short-term social convenience. The process causes no harm. People don't really believe their stereotype descriptions or those of others."

    a. Do you agree or disagree? Why?

    b. Can stereotyping be eliminated?

9. a. Review the 13 examples of sex typing.

    b. Identify those with which you fully agree, partially agree, do not agree.

    c. Discuss each, giving the reasons for your feelings.

10. a. Review the several objections and responses to the issue of women in management.

    b. Which objections do you feel are more valid, less valid?

    c. Why?

11. a. Identify and briefly discuss other forms of prejudicial behavior practiced by business.

    b. In your judgment which should have highest priority for attack and resolution? Why?

12. a. What role should government(s) have in dealing with prejudice by business?

    b. Specifically, what should government(s) do?

13. a. Are you for or against the Equal Rights Amendment? Why?

    b. If passed, what short-term and long-term effects do you feel it will have?

14. How do you react to the recommendations concerning "Equal Opportunity in Business and Industry" for women presented at the end of the chapter?

Suggested Class Projects

1. Visit or write the local office of the EEOC.

    a. Develop a complete description for the processing of a discrimination-based complaint.

    b. Be certain to include estimates of time and costs.

    c. Prepare a schematic (flow chart) of the process so that your findings can be easily communicated to your colleagues.

    d. Use your research as the basis for a group discussion and critical evaluation of the complaint resolution process.

2. a. Interview at least 10 people in the 18 to 26 year old bracket and a like number over age 50.

    b. Your short questionnaire should be aimed at learning the perceptions and attitudes toward working women.

    c. Note and discuss differences and similarities between these two groups.

3. Perform your own analysis of a local large company.

    a. Attempt to learn the ratio of women to men at various levels, job classifications, and pay rates.

b. Interview top management representatives and personnel executives to learn their opinions and policies concerning women in business.

c. In your judgment does the company appear to practice what it preaches? Support your conclusions.

d. Develop a set of action recommendations that you feel the company should adopt.

4. a. Organize an informal group discussion on the topic, "Women's Place."

b. Be certain women and men are equally represented.

c. Tape record the entire session.

d. Analyze the tapes. What conclusions do you reach?

5. a. Select individuals from several of the so-called minority groups. Group membership may be based on religion, national origin, sex, race, economic status, etc.

b. Interview one person from each group you select. Ask them to identify (and rank if possible) our society's most serious problems involving prejudice and discrimination.

c. Ask your respondents what part they feel business plays in problems of discrimination.

d. What recommendations do your respondents have to improve the situation?

6. a. Investigate "affirmative action programs" and the related "quota system" prescribed by the federal government.

b. Secure and critique copies of the regulations.

Supplementary Readings

Articles

Adams, Alan E. "New Guidelines on Sex Discrimination." *Banking,* June 1972, p. 16.
Boyle, Barbara M. "Equal Opportunity for Women is Smart Business." *Harvard Business Review* (May-June 1973): 85-95.
"Double Standard." *New Republic,* May 29, 1971, p. 12.
"Employment: Women's Gains." *Newsweek,* January 11, 1971, p. 70.
"Equal Opportunities." *New Republic,* October 30, 1971, p. 10.
Freeman, Richard B. "Decline of Labor Market Discrimination and Economic Balance." *American Economic Association Journal* 63 (1973): 280-295.
"Frontal Assault on Male Chauvinism." *Broadcasting,* January 18, 1971, p. 34.
Gray, Betty MacMorran. "Economics of Sex Bias." *The Nation,* June 14, 1971, pp. 742-744.
Gruchow, Nancy. "Discrimination: Women Charge Universities, Colleges with Bias." *Science,* May 1970, pp. 559-561.
"Guidelines for Complying With Equal Employment Practices." *Banking,* July 1970, pp. 54-56.
Heilman, Joan Rattner. "Custom-made Jobs for Mothers." *Parent's Magazine,* January 1973, p. 56.
"How Bosses Feel About Women's Lib." *Business Week,* June 13, 1970, pp. 98-100.
"I Didn't Raise My Girl to be a Soldier: Sense and Nonsense About ERA." *Christian Century,* October 25, 1972. p. 1056.

MBA. March 1973 issue, the majority of which is devoted to the description of career problems facing female MBA degree holders.
"Motherhood vs. the Job." *McCalls,* May 1971, p. 43.
Munts, Raymond, and Weiss, David C. "Women Workers: Protection or Equality?" *Industrial and Labor Relations,* October 1970, p. 3.
Peterson, Gary G., and Bryant, Linda. "Eliminating Sex Discrimination — Who Must Act." *Personnel Journal* (1972): 587-591.
"Progress in the Role of Women is Steady and It's Sure." *U.S. News and World Report,* May 14, 1973, pp. 66-69.
"Report of the Status of Women." *McCalls,* September 1970, p. 128.
Rossi, Alice. "Job Discrimination and What Women Can Do About It." *Atlantic Monthly,* March 1970, pp. 99-102.
"Russia — Equal at Work." *The Economist,* May 22, 1971, p. 37.
Schein, Virginia. "Implications and Obstacles to Full Participation of the Woman Worker." *Best's Review,* April 1972, p. 22. Life/Health Insurance edition.
Seligman, Daniel. "How 'Equal Opportunity' Turned Into Employment Quotas." *Fortune,* March 1973, p. 160.
"Sex Guidelines for Federal Contractors." *The Office,* December 1970, p. 20
Sherrill, Robert. "That Equal Rights Amendment — What, Exactly, Does it Mean?" *New York Times Magazine,* September 20, 1970, p. 25.
Sinowitz, Betty E. "New Legal Remedies for Women." *Today's Education,* December 1972, pp. 29-31.
"Slow Gains at Work." *Time,* March 20, 1972, pp. 80-82.
Stull, Richard Alan. "New Answers to an Old Question: Women's Place in the What?" *Personnel Journal* (Jan. 1973): 31-35.
"Up the Job Ladder — Gains for Women." *U.S. News and World Report,* October 2, 1972, pp. 44-46.
"Women Profs Fight Back." *Newsweek,* May 17, 1971, pp. 99-102.
"Women's Liberation Counts a Victory." *Business Week,* June 13, 1970, pp. 98-100.
Wright, Douglas. "The Master Discriminatory Tool." *Computers and Automation,* September 1972, pp. 22-23.
"You Still Have a Long Way to Go — Baby." *Business Week,* September 25, 1971, p. 74.
Zellner, Harriet. "Discrimination Against Women, Occupational Segregation and the Relative Wage." *American Economic Review.* May 1972, p. 157.

7

Man Versus Mangroves

After a long silence one of the men spoke, "They're like a string of emeralds set in a sea of crystal. It never fails to excite me, such beauty within sight of downtown Miami."

A brown pelican folded its wings and split the clean sea air from 75 yards up. Hundreds of silvery pilchards squirted from the water an instant before the plummeting predator's shadow darkened the subsurface world. The pelican surfaced, tilted his head, and lazily emptied his full bill into his stomach.

"Bonefish — fifty yards — eleven o'clock" the fishing guide whispered. His voice trembled a bit as it always did when he spotted a bonefish tail glistening as it splashed above the surface in the bright morning sun.

The guide skillfully poled the skiff across the clear and quiet sand flat. "Fish — forty feet! Ten o'clock — cast!" Suddenly the fish exploded, ignited its afterburner, and sped off the flat into the deeper water of south Biscayne Bay.

"What happened?" the guide asked. The man from Chicago, apparently deep in thought, looked up.

"Sorry, I guess I wan't paying much attention. How many of those islands are there anyway?"

"Well, there are five small keys called the Ragged Keys. Then, there's Boca Chita, Sands, and Elliott Key. These islands are pretty good size. Elliott Key is about eight miles long."

"How close to the mainland is Elliott?"

"It's about eight miles across the bay from Homestead, but the only way to get there is by boat. I guess that's why the Keys are still so unspoiled — not many people can get to them. Thank God for that. If those old mangrove trees could talk they would really tell a story. They've seen it all. They were here when the Indians used to fish these waters. They watched the Spanish fleets, heavy with Aztec gold, shatter against the reefs."

"That's just the trouble, don't you see?" the man from Chicago replied. "These islands would be fantastic if only people *could* get to them."

The Chicagoan wasn't just passing the time of day. He was president of a large and very successful real estate development corporation. His company specialized in taking "raw" land, clearing it, and creating entire new communities complete with homes, apartments, shopping centers, recreational facilities, and industry. The corporation had been particularly successful with projects carved out of wilderness but with reasonable access to urban centers. Their projects in Colorado, Oregon, California, and the Carolinas had all received national recognition. Institutional investors anxiously waited to invest millions in planned future ventures.

"Perhaps this fishing trip wasn't a waste of time after all."

"What do you mean?" the guide queried.

"Well, I've been kind of scouting for a new project, and I think I've found it. Of course there will be a lot of problems, but time and money will take care of them. First, we'll get the state to build a toll causeway from Key Biscayne connecting Miami and these Keys. The smaller islands will be developed as exclusive resorts. Boca Chita Key is perfect for condominium high-rises. Of course Elliott presents unlimited potential. At least two, perhaps three, resort-based communities, each with its own yacht club, marina, golf course, and country club, surrounded by townhouses. The waterfront property on the Atlantic side of the island will be perfect for high rise condos. I'll predict ten thousand people on Elliott Key alone! Hell, with this energy thing people from the North will flock to this project like sheep. You know, it may be possible to link up Key Largo by bridge. Think of it — one continuous resort, retirement, and recreation based community from Miami to Key West!"

"Not before lunch," the guide answered quietly.

"You can take me in now," the developer said.

"But we've only just got here," replied the guide.

"Don't worry — you'll get your money!" snapped the impatient executive.

As the guide silently poled his skiff off the flat to deeper water he felt a little sick and a little sad. He thought deeply to himself, "How long can this last? What chance do mangroves have against man?"

Development — Its Dimensions

The business of development is gargantuan. No one really knows how much money is spent or produced as a result of development activities. The reason is that real estate development cuts across many and varied lines of business activity. Development activity begins with studies of present and future needs of potential customers and "ends" with the completion of a housing subdivision, apartment buildings, an office complex, a shopping center, a recreational complex, etc. Actually, in many cases the development process doesn't really "end" in the economic sense. Developed projects must be managed, and the pay-off period usually extends decades into the future.

Thus the impact of development activity is considerable. Who gets in on the act? This varies by project. But the following list is somewhat representative.

1. Entrepreneur. The basic drive to engage in development activity is supplied by the energetic businessman. This individual looks out on the world with an imaginative and prophetic eye, able to visualize future needs and conceptualize how they might be fulfilled.

2. Real Estate professionals. These individuals or syndicates appraise the development idea. If it has potential, the real estate "pros" will often work with the entrepreneur(s) throughout the entire project, from the acquisition of the raw land to the sale and even management of finished units.

3. Technical specialists. A host of specialties is covered by this designation. Attorneys, accountants, and architects are needed to formalize agreements, prepare financial analyses, and draft plans for structures. Market researchers, appraisers, economic analysts, promotional firms, consulting engineers, etc., may be retained to provide expertise in their areas of competence.

4. Money lenders. Most development projects require large sums of money. Funds are needed for research, plan formulation, and land optioning or acquisition. If this "seed" money results in a viable project the next major need is for construction money. Finally, permanent financing is sought. This is usually in the form of long-term mortgages similar in concept to the mortgage on your home. Institutions interested in financing development activities include banks, savings and loans, real estate investment trusts, pension funds, insurance companies, mortgage banking firms, investor syndicates, the government, and others.

5. The building trades. Building contractors, their subcontractors, skilled tradesmen, plumbers, electricians, heavy equipment operators, masons, semiskilled and unskilled construction laborers, etc., are now needed to turn the plans into reality.

6. Suppliers. A wide variety of businesses depend on development activity for their own livelihood. The list of building materials suppliers alone is a long one — just look in the yellow pages! In addition, other businesses are involved such as nursery firms, landscapers, parking lot paving companies, etc.

7. Marketing. The development must be sold to potential clients. Marketing activity begins by defining present and future unfulfilled needs, which translate into development opportunity. Projects may then be designed around these needs. Mass communication (advertising and sales promotion) and personal communication (personal selling) programs must be designed. Pricing strategies and decisions must be made. Finally, customer problems, complaints, or other additional requirements must be handled.

8. Ongoing operation and management. Manpower and materials are needed to operate the completed apartment complex, office building, shopping center, recreational facility, etc. Often the developer will separate from the project at this point. Ongoing project operation may be turned over to a subsidiary firm, another business organization, or the tenants.

The development cycle is somewhat self-perpetuating. The developer leaves the completed project and looks for new potential and the cycle begins again.

It's important to note how development activity permeates the economic strata of the area affected. The scope and breadth of development means jobs and income for the professional C.P.A., attorney, engineer, etc., as well as for the common laborer. In addition to those directly involved in a "hands-on" way in the development activity, scores of direct and indirect suppliers benefit. Even those who have no knowledge about the development activity may profit. For example, a retired worker in California may enjoy a cost of living escalation in his pension check made possible by the interest income earned on an apartment complex financed by his pension fund. Finally, the ultimate clients benefit. They have attractive and modern new homes, offices, shopping, or recreational facilities. Children are born, roots are set down, and a once vacant area becomes deeply rooted in the lives of hundreds of thousands of people.

Development — Is Bigger Better?

It almost sounds patriotic, doesn't it? Well, to some extent growth and development have been an integral part of our society's objectives. "Raw" (undeveloped) land was hostile. Our forefathers fought nature, cleared the land, and settled the country. Almost everyone liked the economic spinoffs and the civilizing effect of growth and urbanization. The best way to ensure the continued flow of opportunity, jobs, and incomes was to continue developing.

Now, however, the shibboleth "the bigger the better" is beginning to be questioned by many. Doubts are being expressed concerning the long-term validity of continued growth and development. The Chamber of Commerce boosterism aimed at more in-migration, housing starts, apartment complexes, office buildings, and shopping centers is being toned down by some communities. Terms such as "building moratorium," "strong zoning code," and "no-growth candidate" are seen and heard with increasing frequency.

In Boca Raton, Florida, and Carson City, Nevada, for example, legislation has been passed imposing arbitrary population limits.

In Marin County, California, officials are refusing to make water connections to new buildings.

In San Jose, California, a city that doubled in size to 500,000 persons in the past decade, you have to get permission from the local school board before you can build a house.

Already, Vermont, Hawaii, and Oregon have passed statewide laws limiting population growth, and several other states are expected to follow suit.

Oregon Governor Tom McCall made headlines in 1971 when he told Americans to "visit Oregon but, for heaven's sake, don't come here to live." A year later he said, "Don't even visit."

One state on the verge of adopting restrictive "no-grow" or "slow-grow" legislation is Colorado, "where powerful civic and political forces are at work in Denver, Boulder, Colorado Springs, and other communities in the fertile and populous strip on the western flank of the Rockies."[1]

As you might expect, the antidevelopment forces are not without opposition. The benefits of development are many. Like most controversial issues in the business/society interface there are excellent cases to be made on both sides.

"All of this has not been without conflict. In Colorado, and elsewhere, the no-grow movement has been fought bitterly by businessmen, developers, and labor unions, particularly those in the construction trades.

In the middle, and often subject to abuse from both sides, are the slow-grow advocates."[2]

The growth and development dilemma is one which will affect all of us directly or indirectly now and in the future. This issue brings into play several conflicting values. The problem becomes even more perplexing when you consider that for each individual there are some potentially desirable outcomes as well as potential undesirable outcomes related to growth and development.

The remainder of this chapter will serve as a point of departure from which you can think about, analyze, discuss, and debate this unique problem area. In an effort to introduce this broad topic area you will be deeply immersed in an actual situation. Remember, please, that there are several aspects of the growth-development issue. The case presented is only a point of departure. The topic is much too broad and complex to be covered completely in one chapter or one book.

[1] "We Don't Want You. Go Away," *The Miami Herald*, October 14, 1973. *Note:* Boulder, Denver, and Colorado Springs are on the eastern slope of the Continental Divide, not the western slope.

[2] "We Don't Want You. Go Away."

Coral Gables — Paradise of Prosperity

The following case situation could have happened anywhere. In fact, situations like this are developing throughout the country. The events you are about to consider happened in Coral Gables, Florida, from approximately 1967 through 1975.

Coral Gables is situated south of downtown Miami. Its principal "industries" include the University of Miami, with approximately 16,000 students and a staff of 4,500, and close to 45 corporation branch headquarters for Latin American operations. The following excerpt from a City of Coral Gables Community Development Department pamphlet portrays the "Gables" mood.

> Ask a Gableite what Coral Gables means to him and his answer may be: "Gracious Living." That's a phrase you hear often in the Gables — "gracious living" in "the city planned for perfect living." To strangers there is a promotional ring to those words. So you dig deeper. Ask Gableites to define and amplify what they mean and you begin to realize there is more to Coral Gables than clichés, opulent homes, immaculate lawns, flourishing tropical shrubbery and winding Spanish-named streets.
>
> "Well," said a young matron from Philadelphia, "I guess you'd say that living in the Gables is like belonging to an exclusive club. It's a way of life all its own."
>
> The city jealously guards its blend of the best of past and present. An elaborate but unobtrusive system of checks and safeguards protects Coral Gables' more tangible investments as well as its way of life.
>
> The building code is strict. No building may be erected without the approval of the city's Board of Architects. Construction must harmonize. High standards are maintained pushing the value of Gables property up and up and up...
>
> Typical of Coral Gables is the fact that most homes are luxurious but restrained. Wealth is not flaunted. Homes vary in value from $25,000 to $1 million but virtually all bear the stamp of quiet dignity and rock-like permanence.
>
> The Gables is a city secure in its wealth and social prestige. No Gableite would dream of describing his city in the fabulous superlatives of other Gold Coast communities. To the Gableite, elegance and simplicity are almost synonymous. His parties are relaxed, informal — but rarely develop into prolonged revelry. He enjoys the expensive car at his front door and the sleek cabin cruiser tied up to his canal dock in back. But you may be sure that neither is mink-lined nor gold-plated.[3]

Another City of Coral Gables booklet expands on the general themes already expressed.

---

[3] "Florida's Showcase Community — Coral Gables," obtained from the City of Coral Gables Community Development Department. This profusely illustrated pamphlet is undated and the pages unnumbered.

Coral Gables had a master plan so detailed in its design and so rigidly controlled in its development that the beautiful complexion of the City remains virtually unchanged in concept almost a half century after its founding.

Today, when the "new town" concept of community development is the foremost guideline of professional city planners, Coral Gables is most often cited for the foresight of its founder whose pre-planning has withstood the test of time and whose community has blossomed into one of the most beautiful modern cities in the world.

Named after George Merrick's homestead which still stands on Coral Way, Coral Gables was blue-printed to emulate the elegant atmosphere of South European country estates. Private homes as well as public buildings were required to follow a Mediterranean architectural theme, while well-manicured public gardens with fountains and shaded footpaths introduced a charm that even today is unique. Towering entrance-ways located on the City's main thoroughfares extend a gracious welcome to residents and visitors alike.

Today, even the most modern building blends harmoniously with the older structures. Overseeing this is the Coral Gables Board of Architects which must pass approval on all designs.

Strict zoning regulations protect all neighborhoods in the City, insure consistently high quality and guarantee property investments in the future.[4]

Even allowing for the permissible puffery normally associated with promotional literature almost everyone would agree that the Gables is a delightful place to live, study, and work. Its some 7,000 acres stretch from the shores of Biscayne Bay inland. An outstanding school system and high quality city services are additional plusses for the 43,000 people who call the Gables home.

Paradise in Peril?

In December of 1967 an event occurred which has had profound effects on this quiet South Florida community. Situated along Biscayne Bay and stretching inland is a tract of land of approximately 500 acres. This tract is referred variously as the "Cocoplum tract," "Cocoplum beach property," or simply "Cocoplum." On December 18, 1967, the *Coral Gables Times* quietly noted that 11 tracts comprising 482.89 acres on the Metro (Metropolitan Dade County) tax rolls had been sold for $2,264,560. Someone had purchased the entire Cocoplum tract.

The Cocoplum tract was highly regarded by ecologists. Its mangrove

---

[4]"Corporate Capital of the Americas/Coral Gables, Fla." This publication seeks to acquaint business firms with the advantages a Gables location offers. It describes transportation, banking, labor, education, cultural facilities, living conditions, utilities, and government. The publication is undated and pages are unnumbered.

shoreline and wooded interior stood out in sharp contrast to the nearby urban environment. The shallow grass flats immediately offshore served as a nursery for shrimp, crabs, fishes, and other salt water fauna and flora important in the aquatic food chain. A later story in the *Miami Herald* was headlined "Skunks, Possum, Fox, Anteater Among Cocoplum's Displaced."[5] Birds of many types found the Cocoplum tract an idyllic haven. People were largely absent from the tract. Only one uninhabited old building interrupted the natural environment. This small building was valued at $1,200 and was not visible to those enjoying the tract's wild state.

The inland side of Cocoplum was bordered by the charming two-laned Old Cutler Road. "Old Cutler" is graced by beautiful homes, lawns, and landscaping. In some areas the branches of huge banyan trees touch above the roadway and form a natural leafy tunnel. Old Cutler, although extremely busy during the commuting rush hours, is the type of road on which one drives for the pleasure of driving and experiencing unique, natural, subtropical beauty.

The sale of Cocoplum to a group of private investors all but ended the procrastination of Gables government officials who "were considering" the development of Cocoplum for the public. Note a quotation from City minutes:

"The City Managers presented plans for a recreation area designated as"Cocoplum Park" located south of Cartegena Plaza between Granada Boulevard and Old Cutler Road, and owned by the Miami Corporation. The City Manager was instructed to forward the proposed sketch to the Miami Corporation and to enter into negotiation for an agreement on use of the land for such recreational purpose, if feasible and practicable.[6]

What a shock it was when the Coral Gables Planning and Zoning Board received a request from the new owners of Cocoplum for substantial rezoning that would facilitate a massive development and create a new city within a city for thousands of new residents. The request clearly indicated the extent of the developer's plans for Cocoplum.[7]

---

[5]*The Miami Herald*, October 29, 1973.

[6]Minutes, City Commission of Coral Gables, June 22, 1965.

[7]See "Exhibit B, Owners Affidavit for Changes of Zoning," June 17, 1968, Cocoplum Files. *Note:* Much of the material for the remainder of the chapter was based on research of public documents in the "Cocoplum files." These files are available at the offices of the Zoning Department, third floor, Coral Gables City Hall. There are approximately ten files covering 1965 through the present. Documents are filed in approximate date order, but no page numbers are assigned.

Details of Owners' Request for Zoning Changes — Cocoplum 1968

Tract	Size (acres)	Proposed Utilization	Units	Density units per acre
A	160	18-hole Golf Course & Club		
B	2.8	Single Family Residences	5 lots	
C	8.6	Townhouses	69	8
D	11.2	Townhouses	70	8
E	21.7	Garden Apartments	304	14
F	9.5	Garden Apartments	133	14
G	5.8	Medium Rise Apartments	174	30
H	6.2	High-Rise Apartments	310	50
I	5.5	Medium Rise Apartments	155	30
J	4.9	High Rise Apartments	245	50
K	7.1	High Rise Apartments	355	50
L	7.7	Beach Club		
M	7.8	High Rise	390	50
N	5.1	High Rise	255	50
O	7.4	Medium Rise	222	30
P	8.6	Marina		
Q	5.4	Shops		
R	7.6	Garden Apartments	106	14
S	8.3	Garden Apartments	116	14
T	13.5	Garden Apartments	189	14
U	23.5	Garden Apartments	329	14
V	22.6	Garden Apartments	316	14
W	4.8	Garden Apartments	67	14
X	4.0	Single Family	6	

The details presented are summarized for your convenience.

Summary: Owners' Request for Zoning Changes — Cocoplum, 1968

Type Dwelling	Units
Garden Apartments	1,560
High-rise Apartments	1,555
Medium-rise Apartments	561
Townhouses	158
Single Family (number of lots)	11
Total Units	3,845

One of the themes of the Cocoplum developer's plan called for much open space and high quality recreational facilities. Part of the request for rezoning submitted by the owners, the Miami Corporation, included a land use plan. This plan provided some details concerning open space, recreational facilities, and planned living units.

Land Use Plan Description of Cocoplum Facilities

Facility	General Description
1. Golf and Country Club	Approximately 160 acre championship course and related facilities comparable in quality to Coral Gables and Riviera country clubs.
2. Marina	All facilities. Restrictions include only limited boat repairs permitted, no boat ramp or launching facilities. (Author's note: this keeps the small boater with trailerable boats out and also eliminates transient small boaters.)
3. Beach Club	Swimming, playground, etc.
4. Yacht Club	Membership limited to residents and country club members.
5. Shops	Neighborhood shops zoning class "CA" (1,250 sq. ft.)
6. Single Family Homes	Class R-14 (2,500 sq. ft.)
7. Garden Apartments	Surrounding golf course, 3 stories.
8. Townhouses	Singly owned, 900 sq. ft. minimum size, approximately 40 feet.
9. Medium-Rise Apartments	Rental units, 8 stories
10. High-Rise Apartments	(No height specified by developers, city zoning restrictions specify a 13-story limit)

The Battle Lines are Drawn

The reaction of many Gables citizens to the proposed development of Cocoplum from a subtropical wilderness to a new luxury community of approximately 7,500 residents was immediate and intense. As required by law, a public hearing was held to facilitate a discussion of the Cocoplum proposal. This meeting and subsequent meetings can be described in a word — wild! Citizens' groups reacted quickly, and local media began in-depth coverage of Cocoplum.

> Principal opposition for the plan has come from the Citizens League, the Sunrise Harbour Association and such individuals as Cliff Gould, former president of both the South Ponce Improvement Association and the Sunrise Harbor Association...
> One person who feels that the ambitious plan by Henry C. Rexach, representing a group of Puerto Rico Investors, is every Gableites business, however, is Ms. James Jude... She felt that the size of the project and its overall effect on the Gables makes it everybody's concern.
> "If monied interests have the power to change zoning there is no security for any one in Coral Gables," she said.
> Mrs. Jude's husband is president of both the Sunrise Harbor group and the Citizens League.

Values in Conflict

These groups favor that the property be developed as it is zoned — single family or acquired by the City for a public park and marina.[8]

Support for the Cocoplum developers was also evident in the media and in letters received by city government:

> I have had the opportunity to review the master plan carefully that is being presented for consideration. I would like to go on record as having no objection to it. It is imaginative; it has been carefully thought out with proper screening, which should afford all the adjoining areas suitable protection; and, at the same time, it sets forth clearly the highest and best use for the land.
>
> The group of persons insisting that this tract be taken over by the City of Coral Gables, creating a park, some sort of wildlife preserve and retaining Tahiti Beach are not concerning themselves with the economics of the matter. There are sufficient parks in the area to take care of the needs of everyone. Their idea of developing of this tract could easily result in higher taxes for each and every resident of the Gables. On the other hand, proper development of the tract would result in a substantial increase of taxable property which could easily and should reduce the taxes of every resident...[9]

The Gables is home base for 45 Latin American headquarters of major corporations. A prominent corporation executive voiced his opinion as both a private citizen and a corporation representative:

> ...to change this zoning now would alter drastically the character of the surrounding area and be grossly unfair to the nearby homeowners. The result would be a high density, transient, non-home owner area with large patches of commercialism. Obviously, this would be a traffic bother... the bridge would have to be rebuilt and Old Cutler Road widened to four lanes. What a shame to destroy all their beauty!
>
> Certainly the speculators and developers interested in this large tract were well aware that it has been zoned single family residential. Why should they be able to reap a windfall at the expense of those who built their homes nearby in good faith?
>
> Both as a private individual and an officer of Esso Inter-America, Inc. I have heartily recommended Coral Gables as a place to work and live to international companies considering locating here. One of the strong factors that has made Coral Gables great is its excellent zoning and strict building codes. Please keep Coral Gables the City Beautiful. Don't destroy one of the more beautiful residential areas in the U.S.[10]

In January 1969, the Miami Corporation sold the tract: "'483 acres were

---

[8]*Coral Gables Times,* August 12, 1968.

[9]"Cocoplum file — City of Coral Gables" This letter was written by a mortgage company president who owns multiple properties in an area adjacent to the Cocoplum tract.

[10]This letter was from the Corporate Secretary of Esso Inter-American, Inc. This Coral Gables citizen and business leader had recently purchased a home in a tract adjacent to Cocoplum. He also stated that those he had consulted were also against the zoning changes.

sold for $3,950,000 or about $8,195 per acre. The buyers were Crow, Pope & Carter, Orlando apartment builders, and Cocoplum Associates headed by Puerto Rican investor H. C. Rexach. Selling the land for all cash was the Miami Corporation...."[11]

The acquisition by Crow, Pope & Carter introduced a new variable into the rapidly heating controversy. Crow, Pope & Carter are reputable and experienced developers. They are a highly specialized corporate group with a record of success and an ability to accomplish their objectives.

The original land use plan had been withdrawn as a result of the furor it created. The land use plan was now being redesigned to make it more acceptable. Voluntary plan withdrawal was probably not only motivated by good will. Gables law requires that a one-year minimum period elapse before formerly rejected plans may be resubmitted for new consideration.

The Plot Thickens

As if the Cocoplum development controversy was not enough to keep interested parties and Gables government at a fever pitch, the following bombshell hit in November 1969:

> The largest single land deal in Coral Gables history — a 650 acre tract on Biscayne Bay untouched for more than 40 years — has been closed by one of the world's largest hotel chains for ultimate development as a fashionable resort hotel-golf course complex.
> ITT-Sheraton Hotels paid $7.5 million dollars — or about $12,458 per acre — for the last remaining chunk of Deering Estate in the Gables.
> ...an ITT-Sheraton spokesman in Boston confirmed that the development would include a resort hotel, two 18-hole golf courses, a marina and possibly adjoining apartments but not homes.
> ...Russo [the Miami attorney involved in the transaction] said that development would have to start within five years.
> "The property is too valuable to just sit on for too long."
> He [Russo] also said the corporation is not stressing high density to maximize its initial investment. Rather, he said, the hotel resort would be designed to attract wealthy tourists and international corporate gatherings.
> The importance of this purchase and its potential impact on land use and Coral Gables politics is evidenced in the following statement:
> "The Sheraton purchase and the Cocoplum development just to the north represent more than 1,000 acres of land — about a seventh of the city's entire acreage.[12]

Cocoplum Development Plan — Down But Not Out

The modified Cocoplum development plan was rejected by the Gables planning and zoning board. The developers promptly appealed their nega-

[11]*The Miami Review,* January 9, 1969.
[12]*Coral Gables Times,* November 17, 1969.

tive decision to the city commission. The following quotations concisely summarize the events:

> ...three members of the Planning and Zoning Board favored the 500-acre residential and recreational project, while two members voted against the zoning changes... But that was enough to kill the plan because more than 20 per cent of the neighboring property owners objected, making a four-fifths vote necessary for approval.... The plan will be appealed to the city commission, where a four-fifths vote also will be required.... If it fails there, Cocoplum Associates, Inc. must wait another year before submitting a revised plan.... Hundreds of property owners opposed the development at a five-hour zoning hearing...[13]

Another paper reported: "... by a 3-2 vote, the city fathers [City Commission] decided to let the Zoning Board give a recommendation on all 500 acres involved in what could be the largest land development plan in the city's history."[14]

During this game of political football, the City Commission passed a resolution worth noting. Resolution #15305 waived the 12-month minimum period for resubmission of rejected zoning requests. The door remained open for the Cocoplum developers.

Cocoplum — Yes!

During the Cocoplum debate and in the ensuing several months before the developers submitted a new revised plan, both sides remarshalled their forces and attempted to develop factual evidence that would yield an ultimate result in their favor. The developers cited several reasons why Coral Gables should grant the requested zoning variances and approve the land use plan. These reasons included:

1. An increased tax base — Cocoplum would produce an estimated $1.5 million in additional tax revenue. On a cost-benefit basis, this amount would be considerably higher than the costs of additional city services required by Cocoplum residents. In 1968, Cocoplum tax revenue was $50,000. By 1980, the Cocoplum development would produce $3 million.

2. Compatible density — Although initial density figures appear high it must be remembered that the plan calls for a 160 acre golf complex, marina, beach club, and yacht club. Actual density, i.e., units per acre, is no greater than Gables' present density. In fact, Cocoplum density is less than already existing Gables apartment projects.

3. Socio-economic class of residents — Cocoplum will not attract buyers or renters seeking a cheap residence. Prices will be high enough to minimize transients. The area will likely be populated by professionals,

[13]*The Miami Herald,* November 25, 1969.
[14]*Coral Gables Times,* December 18, 1969.

semi-professionals, executives, and retired individuals. Most residents will be older. There will be no problem with small children.

4. Traffic congestion — Rush hour traffic is already overloading existing roadways. With or without Cocoplum, roads will soon need to be widened and access to the north, Miami Beach, etc., improved. The development of Cocoplum will hasten these sorely needed improvements.

5. General economic impact — The development and building of Cocoplum will provide jobs and income for Dade County families. In addition, scores of industries and individual businesses will benefit in the short-run developmental phase. After the project is completed, its residents will provide an ongoing increase in business activity and the economic base of Coral Gables.

6. Current plan is only alternative — While the per acre price may make it appear that the developers "stole" the property, acquisition of raw land is only the beginning. Raw land must be surveyed, cleared, utilities installed, roads cut, canals dug and bulkheaded, etc. This work is funded by the developer and comprises a large part of development expense. In order to earn a reasonable return for their efforts, Cocoplum must be developed with multi-family zoning.

"Development of the Cocoplum tract as 'single family' in its entirety is not commerciably feasible nor is it in the best interest of Coral Gables."[15]

Further support for the economic feasibility argument came from the president of the real estate firm that developed nearby Gables Estates, 216 acres of waterfront single-family lots: "Thank you for your recent inquiry relative to our experience in the development and sale of the Gables Estates property. In my opinion, such a development as Gables Estates with entirely single family houses would not today be economically feasible. The cost of bulkheading, filling, the loss of land needed to supply the fill, as well as the length of time required for completion and sale of lots, would preclude such a development as Gables Estates from being a profitable undertaking."

7. Elimination of nuisance — To many, undeveloped property in the midst of an urban setting produces undesirable side effects.

The following quote is extracted from a letter submitted by a Gables resident living near the Cocoplum tract. This citizen felt that the proposed development was: "Much better than present weeds, mosquitoes, sandflies, foxes, skunks, rats, motorcycle love-ins, the neighborhood now endures."

Developers Submit New Plan

In response to massive public pressure and a mixed reaction from city

[15]Testimony of Reinhold P. Wolff, economic consultant, before the Coral Gables Planning and Zoning Board, November 19, 1969. The Cocoplum consultant's full report, supporting the developers, is contained in the Cocoplum file.

124 *Values in Conflict*

government, the developers retreated. On April 17, 1970, the revised plan was submitted to city government.[16] Highlights of the revised plan include:

1. Voluntary deed restrictions — Guaranteeing that the golf course would remain a golf course and not later be developed for other purposes.

2. A dramatic increase in single family housing — The initial plan called for 7 acres equaling about 11 building lots dedicated to single family residence. The revised plan called for 147 acres equaling about 250 single family homesites. This raised single family acreage to about 30% of the total Cocoplum plan.

3. Townhouses eliminated — The Gables had no townhouse ordinance. The developers eliminated the problem by eliminating the dwellings. Single family lots were located around the golf course (and elsewhere), occupying much of the space previously reserved for townhouses.

4. Substantial changes in multi-family structures — Only 19% of the now 497-acre development will be zoned multi-family. This will include:

a. 20 acres, garden apartments, 35 feet high, 17.9 units per acre.

b. 75 acres for apartments, 79 feet high, 6 living stories plus 2 lower level parking, 28.6 units per acre.

5. Improved parking — Planned parking facilities will exceed that called for in the Coral Gables city code.

6. Recreational facilities — The following detail was presented:

Description	Acres
a. parking, open space, swimming pools	75
b. golf and country club	133.8
c. yacht and beach club	14.2
d. yacht basin and facilities	19.4
e. waterways	67.9
f. landscaped parkway (entrance boulevard)	20.2
Total planned open spaces & recreational facilities in acres	330.5

The revised land use plan zoning mix is summarized below:

Type of Structure	Units
single family homesites	250
garden apartments	353
apartments	2,147
Total units	2,750

Approximately 5.5 units per acre

7. Other strong points of the revised plan:

---

[16]The complete plan is referred as "3753-2" and may be examined in the Zoning Office Cocoplum file No. 7.

a. Cocoplum's density, computed as 10.8 persons per acre, yields an estimated population of 5,400.

b. The "Blue Ribbon Committee" appointed by the city to objectively study the development question defined low density as not exceeding 12 persons per acre. Cocoplum complies with that definition.[17]

c. Even with the apartments, Cocoplum is only 9% above the density of surrounding areas that are single family tracts. This is significant when you consider that adjacent 216 acre "Gables Estates" averages less than one single family home per acre.

d. Cocoplum will result in only 23% net population increase over development of the tract as all single family.

e. Development within existing single family zoning will eliminate hundreds of acres of open space and much needed recreational facilities. The result would be 497 acres filled with houses.

Mr. Gerald Kravetz, P.E., managing partner for Crow, Pope & Carter, concluded his firm's new proposal by stating: "...The importance of proper development of Cocoplum to the City, as well as us, is uppermost in our minds.... We have attempted in this plan to make every possible effort to protect the bayfront, minimize density, and evolve a plan which will be second to none in total community planning. This we feel we have accomplished."

Cocoplum — No!

One of the most vocal and effective organizations fighting to defeat the Cocoplum proposal was the Citizens League, Inc. of Coral Gables. A circular distributed to Gables residents concisely summarizes the major objections to the Cocoplum project.

> Dear Gables Residents:
> Vote against re-zoning the Cocoplum properties for the following reasons:
> Preserve the zoning integrity of the Gables. It is our prime asset, and sets the Gables apart from other areas.
> The high-rise and medium-rise apartments planned will spoil the natural beauty of the area.
> High density pollutes air and water and attracts undesirable people.
> Traffic on Old Cutler Road will be doubled.
> Our most beautiful roads, LeJeune, Old Cutler, Sunset, and Ingraham, will be four-laned.
> Gables Estates, Old Cutler Bay, and the area east of Snapper Creek Estates will next be re-zoned for apartments because of continuity and the precedent set.

[17]The "Blue Ribbon Committee" ultimately recommended that Cocoplum's original zoning — single family — be retained and that the area be developed only as a single family tract.

The developers make no provision for sewers, water, schools, and parks. They use more taxes than they pay.

Foreign developers and speculators cannot be held to their promises and are only here long enough to increase the value of their property ten-fold and move on to another area.

Appear at the Gables Youth Center of April 22, Easter Day at 8:00 P.M. and let the Zoning Board know your feelings and save Coral Gables!

It would be possible to devote an entire chapter to the detailed objections to Cocoplum. As an alternative, one widely held objection will be presented in some detail. Traffic congestion and the myriad undesirable side effects produced were bound to increase. The developers minimized the problem and did not consider additional traffic a serious drawback.

In an effort to clarify the issues, Gables city government requested the Metro Dade County Department of Traffic and Transportation to study the area and issue a report.[18] The report clearly supported Cocoplum opponents. First, the present traffic flow was calculated.

Present Traffic Flow — Cocoplum Area

Artery	Capacity Vehicles Per Day	Estimated Present Usage	Over-utilization
LeJeune Road	10,000	12,000	2,000
Old Cutler Road	10,000	13,000	3,000
Sunset Road	10,000	8,000	(2,000)
Present Net Overutilization vehicles per day			3,000

Estimated Impact of Cocoplum Traffic — Vehicles per Day

Artery	Minimum	Maximum	Estimated Maximum Impact
LeJeune Road	17,200	19,200	7,200
Old Cutler Road	15,600	16,600	3,600
Sunset Road	13,200	15,200	7,200
Estimated Maximum Cocoplum Impact Over Current Usage — Vehicles per Day			18,000

It is not difficult to understand the concern of Gables residents over the traffic impact of Cocoplum.

In addition to the statistics presented, the traffic report recommended:
1. Four-laning of this area.
2. Construction of additional access to area roads.

[18] A copy of the traffic study may be found in Cocoplum file No. 4. The figures presented are extracted from the report.

3. Modification of an existing traffic circle.
4. Addition of turn bays.
5. Bridge enlargement.
6. Additional grading and crossing areas.

Prior to the scheduled zoning hearing on the revised plan, the *Coral Gables Times* published a short and prophetic editorial. Not only did the editorial forecast a long and bitter fight over Cocoplum, the editor also illustrated sensitivity to the complex national issue which our society will have to deal with time and time again into the indefinite future.

> Whichever decision the Coral Gables City Commission renders Tuesday on the partial re-zoning of the Cocoplum tract, it will not be final.
>
> If it denies the re-zoning request of the developers, Crow, Pope and Carter, the owners are likely to appeal to the Courts.
>
> If the Commission approves the application, then homeowners in adjoining Gables Estates have vowed a court fight.
>
> In a sense, Cocoplum is a microcosm of the wrenching decisions communities are facing everywhere — how to handle the pace of growth without despoiling the amenities of other people, yet not depriving responsible land owners of opportunity to take part in the same growth.[19]

A Continuing Postscript

By now you have every right to know if Cocoplum made it. Well, it isn't that simple. Prior to the zoning hearing the Citizens League got an injunction against the Planning and Zoning Board. The long awaited meeting was cancelled at the last minute. Crow, Pope & Carter showed up, as did scores of citizens who had not heard of the cancellation. The developers distributed sandwiches and drinks while making their pitch to the crowd milling about outside the locked meeting hall. Ultimately, at a later date, the Planning and Zoning Board approved the plan by a 4-to-1 vote. The City Commission approved, by a like margin, the first reading of the rezoning ordinance.

The end? Not quite. Prior to the second reading, the City Commission decided to create another committee to further study Gables development. Some people speculated that pressure from the developers had been successful while supporters of Cocoplum saw this situation from totally opposite point of view. Was it coincidence that city elections were approximately four months off (spring 1971) and that the city fathers continued to stall? A decision for the developers might result in defeat for some city fathers in the coming election.

Several actions and threats of action followed. An effort was made to muster enough support to recall certain City Commissioners. A citywide referendum on Cocoplum was proposed. Mass media advertising was used

[19]*Coral Gables Times,* December 13, 1970.

by each side to plead its case. Charges of corruption, payoffs, and the like were made. There was talk of a probe into Gables government. Court cases were brought beginning with the injunction that blocked the Planning and Zoning Board hearing (later reversed by a higher court) and ended in the Florida Supreme Court.

To a large extent opponents of Cocoplum "won" their victory. What will finally replace the 500 acres of subtropical wilderness and quiet bayside grass flats? No one knows for sure. The following feature story brings you the latest installment of Cocoplum:[20]

> Bowing to pressure from Coral Gables residents — and an edict of the Florida Supreme Court — developers of the controversial Cocoplum tract revealed new plans Monday to build only 450 single family dwellings on the 500-acre tract.
>
> The new plans, which culminate more than four years of zoning battles, a Florida Supreme Court ruling and angry public protest, will make the residential area the "lowest in density in the City," James S. Billings said.
>
> Dr. James Jude, co-founder of the Gables Citizens League and chief opponent of the original high density plan, said he wants to see the plans before he can approve of them, "but the single-family dwellings seem to be acceptable."
>
> Jude said: "The idea, the concept is probably not bad. It's how they're going to do it. They can't disrupt the environment down here."
>
> "There's no question about it that if the county or the state had the money, the land would be better left in its natural state." Jude said. "But Coral Gables will make sure that they [the developers] are tied to their word."
>
> Although the plans have not been finalized and await the decisions of some 26 governmental agencies, Billings said the project is "of the highest planning standards and we anticipate no serious problems."

If you ever get to Miami, be certain to stop at scenic Coral Gables City Hall. There you will receive, at no charge, a Coral Gables self-guided tour map. As you point your car toward the east, I'm sure you'll want to head toward Biscayne Bay between the Coral Gables Waterway and Gables Estates. What will you find?

If you can't get to Miami, look around your own community. You'll probably have no problem finding your own "Cocoplum." If you can't, just wait, it will be "developing" soon.

---

[20]Dorothy K. Gaiter, "Cocoplum to Build Single Family Sites" *The Miami Herald*, October 16, 1973.

Discussion Questions

1. Contrast the values of the Florida fishing guide and the Chicago real estate executive portrayed in the first few pages of the chapter.

2. Prior to the federal government take over, certain Florida Keys islands were privately owned. When the government announced plans to establish the "Biscayne National Monument" some private property owners were incensed. Even though the condemnation awards were generous, some property owners remain embittered by the governmental action that has preserved these islands "for the public."

   a. Do you agree or disagree with the action of Congress in taking land through the process of condemnation? Why? Why not?

   b. Assume the tract of land on which your home is situated is being purchased, at a fair price, by the state as part of a recreational facility expansion. How would you react?

3. a. What benefits does development activity bring to a community and its people?

   b. What undesirable consequences might result from development activity?

   c. In what way(s) might the desirable and undesirable aspects of development be reconciled?

4. React to and discuss this statement: "Since development normally involves millions of dollars it is usually begun by the initiative of wealthy and politically powerful individuals or business organizations. The developer has sophisticated political savvy and topnotch legal and other professional resources. Ultimately, the ordinary citizen can do nothing to prevent the developer from having his way."

5. Discuss the relationships between population growth and development.

6. "Private citizens save their money in various types of institutions, through life insurance purchases, by investing in securities, contributing to pension plans, etc. These pools of money are often reinvested in development activities. Some of the several critics of development ventures actually help to finance them."

   a. To what extent are you interested or aware of the uses made of your savings and/or investments by the recipients of your funds?

   b. In what ways might you impact an investment decision with which you disagree?

7. a. How do you react to the governor of Oregon's remark, "Visit Oregon but, for heaven's sake, don't come here to live."

   b. What about his later revision of that statement to: "Don't even visit"?

8. In spite of the strong language and open pride in the Coral Gables "strict" zoning code, as evidenced in their promotional pamphlet, why do you feel it took approximately six years to kill the Cocoplum proposal?

9. a. How do you feel about the initial Cocoplum land use plan submitted in 1968? What are your reasons?

   b. Analyze the revised plan submitted in 1970. Do you feel it represents an improvement? Why? Why not?

   c. Assume you are a Gables City Commissioner. In light of your familiarity with the Cocoplum project, would you support it?

10. a. What other alternatives to the proposed development of Cocoplum can you suggest?

    b. Which do you favor? Why?

11. Most of the people who opposed Cocoplum were rich. Their fortunes were

made. What did they care that Cocoplum would bring jobs and feed the families of the working man? Sure, it's easy for them to say, "let the people go somewhere else, but I haven't worked in four months and there's no work in sight!"
    a. How would you respond to the construction worker quoted above?
    b. Do you feel the final outcome of the Cocoplum controversy might have been different had the development been proposed for a lower class or middle class area?

12. Analyze and discuss the benefits cited by Cocoplum supporters and the objections raised by the opposition.

13. Compare and contrast the Cocoplum case with a development project in your area.

14. a. "Once established, urban zoning must remain inviolate."
    b. "Zoning is a reflection of the will and needs of the people. It must remain flexible to meet changing conditions."
    c. Which of these two propositions do you support? Why?

Suggested Class Projects

1. a. Contact your local planning/zoning office.
   b. Secure the current zoning regulations and an area zoning map.
   c. Secure copies of the development plans for the area.
   d. Analyze current zoning and plans for future growth.
   e. Present your findings and recommendations.

2. a. Study two or three of the books listed as supplementary readings or other books on development, urban growth, etc.
   b. Summarize the authors' findings and recommendations.
   c. Present your summary to your colleagues.
   d. Note points of agreement and disagreement.
   e. Develop your own or your group's position(s) on the points raised by the various authors.

3. a. Plan a panel presentation. Invite an executive from a real estate development firm, an area planning/zoning official, and a local elected official such as a mayor or city council member.
   b. Ask each to present a 15 minute speech entitled "Recommendations for Future Area Growth."
   c. Conduct open disccussions.
   d. Compare and contrast the points of view presented.
   e. What conclusions do you reach?

4. a. Attempt to locate a development controversy in your area.
   b. Offer your facilities for a forum.
   c. Invite area residents and groups to present their views, pro and con, regarding the development project.
   d. Summarize and analyze the various points of view.
   e. What are your conclusions?

5. a. Develop a research plan to study the following growth-related factors:
     Population
     Traffic
     Crime
     Natural Resources
     Natural Environment

Economic Impact
Overall Quality of Life
   b. Based on your findings, identify the major favorable and/or unfavorable aspects of development on each of the seven factors.
   c. Suggest a system of controls that might reconcile some of the unfavorable aspects and maximize the favorable aspects.
   6. a. Correspond or meet with "no growth" or "slow growth" political candidates.
   b. Analyze their platforms and proposals.
   c. What long-range impact do you believe these candidates/office holders will have? Why?
   7. Some people claim that achievement of a zero population growth rate is *the* basic solution to many of society's problems.
   a. Study "ZPG" literature and the writings of ZPG sympathizers.
   b. Locate material in opposition to ZPG, including religious opposition.
   c. Present your findings and solicit your group's reactions.
   d. What do you conclude? Why?
   8. a. Visit your county's planning department.
   b. Secure copies of the 10-year population projections.
   c. Analyze the data by census tract, age, income level, and any other classification for which there are data available.
   d. What implications are suggested by the data?
   e. What actions, plans, programs, etc., do you suggest in response to the implications noted in "d"?
   9. a. Investigate the totally planned community concept as implemented in Reston, Virginia, or other locations.
   b. Analyze and report about various land use and architectural techniques unique to the planned community concept.
   c. What advantages and disadvantages of the planned community can you identify?

Supplemental Readings

Books

Chapin, F. Stuart, Jr. *Urban Land Use Planning*. Urbana: University of Illinois Press, 1965.

Clawson, Marion, ed. *Modernizing Urban Land Policy*. Baltimore, Md.: Johns Hopkins University Press, 1973.

Delafons, John. *Land-Use Controls in the United States*. Cambridge, Mass.: Harvard University Press, 1962.

Futterman, Robert A. *The Future of Our Cities*. Garden City, N.Y.: Doubleday, 1961.

Greer, Scott. *Urban Renewal and American Cities*. Indianapolis, Ind.: Bobbs-Merrill, 1965.

Grigsby, William. *Housing Markets and Public Policy*. Philadelphia: University of Pennsylvania Press, 1963.

Higbee, Edward. *The Squeeze: Cities Without Space*. New York: William Morrow & Co., 1960.

McCluny, William Ross. *The Environmental Destruction of South Florida.* Coral Gables, Fla.: University of Miami Press, 1969.
Meyerson, Martin; Terrett, Barbara; and Wheaton, William L. C. *Housing, People, and Cities.* New York: McGraw-Hill, 1962.
Murphy, Raymond E. *The American City.* New York: McGraw-Hill, 1966.
Whyte, William H. *The Last Landscape.* Garden City, N.Y.: Doubleday, 19xx.

Articles

"Big Cities Do Have a Future." *U.S. News and World Report,* June 26, 1967, pp. 46-50.
"Condominiums Capture the Florida Market." *Business Week,* November 4, 1972, p. 82.
"Consumerism and the Land Industry: From Marketplace to Political Arena." *Industrial Development and Manufacturers Record* 142 (1973): 24-25.
"Florida Developers Fall Out of Favor." *Business Week.* September 9, 1972, p. 68.
"Growth is a Fighting Word in Colorado's Mountain Wonderland." *Fortune,* October 1973, pp. 148-158.
"Growth? Or No Growth?" *American City,* November 1972, p. 6
"Involving the Citizen in Decision-Making." *Nation's Cities,* May 1968, pp. 11-14.
"Land: The Boom That Really Hurts." *Fortune,* July 1973, pp. 104-109.
"Land Use Battle that Business Faces; Special Report." *Business Week,* August 26, 1972, pp. 40-41.
"A Land Use Freeze Hits Los Angeles." *Business Week,* September 30, 1972, p. 28.
"Land Use Regulations Need Not Be a Bureaucratic Horror Show." *Industrial Development and Manufacturers Record* 142 (1973): 15-17.
"New Town and Urban Change Form." *Land Economics* 48 (1972): 93-103.
"Residential Densities or a Fool's Paradise." *Land Economics* 49 (1973): 1-13.
"Testing the New Land Use Laws." *Business Week,* July 7, 1973, p. 84.

8
The Businessman's View of Social Responsibility

Open communication is the key to developing an understanding of problem situations. The communication is further enriched and the potential for progress enhanced when people meet face-to-face on neutral ground. The position of those communicating and the power they possess to obtain action after decisions are reached are also key discriminators. These conditions were satisfied when approximately 75 businessmen and professors in business and related fields met at the U.C.L.A. Graduate School of Management. For two weeks the participants discussed contemporary challenges in the business-society relationship.

One of the key presentations was given by Fletcher L. Byrom, Chairman of the Board, Kopper's Company, Inc.; Chauncey J. Medberry III, Chairman of the Board, Bank of America; and Martin Stone, Chairman of the Board, Monogram Industries Inc. These executives were asked to discuss the businessman's views of social responsibility. This chapter contains a synthesis of the panel presentation. The remarks emanate from top-level national executive leaders. Each board chairman has current and direct involvement with today's business/society issues. In addition, each of these executives is in a vantage point of high visibility concerning the interface between American society and business.[1]

Social Responsibility — Oversimplification in an Age of Great Complexity

Byrom initiated his remarks by challenging the usefulness of the term "social responsibility." This term is so broad and encompasses so many issues and subtopics that it may not provide the most useful perspective from which to attack the problems under the conceptual umbrella. Byrom quoted Daniel Moynihan, who said that we live in an age of oversimplifiers during an age of great complexity. The current approach to the study and analysis of social responsibility issues has largely been at the macro level.

[1]This chapter is based on: Edward W. Wheatley, "The Businessman's View of Social Responsibility," *Contemporary Challenges in the Business-Society Relationship*, George A Steiner ed., Graduate School of Management, University of California, Los Angeles, 1972, Chapter 5.

Such an approach produces substantial agreement concerning the scope and complexity of the problems. As a result of this conceptual breadth, however, the analyst is plagued with the inability to zero in on specifics and produce an action plan aimed directly at improving upon or solving a definite problem. As an illustration of the overwhelming problems of semantics and emotionalism related to the topic area, Byrom asked if the goal of profit maximization was antisocial. Byrom feels that this concept is simply not consistent. It has been his experience that wealth must be created before it can be allocated. The ability of a firm to earn a profit in and of itself does not carry socially irresponsible implications. Quite the contrary, profits make possible a wide range of technology and resources that can facilitate the correction of many social problems.

Business can earn profits that can be allocated to socially desirable goals both by an individual firm and through the process of taxation. The concept that the costs of solving social problems should be shouldered exclusively by the business community is fallacious. For example, the cost of cleaning up the environment is calculable to the individual whose by-products contribute to environmental damage. These costs can and should be worked into industry pricing structure so that the consumer, as well as the producer, shares the burden created by the desirability of the product.

In addition to the specific subquestion of "Who will pay?" another question arises out of America's objectives relative to work trade. Byrom discussed President Nixon's economic message of 1970. He quoted the president's message stating that other nations were not in the same stage of economic development and were not necessarily as concerned about the environment as the United States. The president felt that since we were emphasizing ecology, United States industry would necessarily incur higher costs of operation. These costs would be due to the money spent on corrective and preventative measures. Such a reallocation of costs in the production sector would reallocate production among other nations. Byrom particularly took issue with Nixon's allegation that such a situation would be good for the world. Would such a situation be good for the steel worker and his family presently unemployed and not likely to find employment in the foreseeable future? Has such a situation been good in the Arizona copper smelting industry where entire firms went out of business while their output was sent to Japan for processing?

Such situations and many related real-life issues indicate the seriousness of the oversimplification syndrome. In such cases it is possible to make the problem go away by utilizing the convenient macro approach. The consequences of the macro approach could be as severe or more severe than the benefits. If this country is to be a free-trade nation, then it must be able to compete realistically with the pricing structures in other economies. Such competition must relate directly to the costs of production that various economies incur and, as such, the individual business firm should not be the only institution to pay for the costs of socially responsible action.

Assuming that the oversimplification syndrome can and will be corrected, American society faces a very difficult task. The entire area of business and society relationships is frought with difficult issues. Byrom raised the question of whether American society is willing to make the tough choices necessary to achieve the goals that critics of business say should be achieved. If it becomes possible to clearly define the issues, two subproblems immediately arise. First, how do we establish priorities among the various problem areas? Second, how does an egalitarian society efficiently choose between alternative courses of action concerning issues where strong and powerful advocates vie on both sides of the question for favorable and sometimes opposite treatment? Byrom reiterated his basic concern for clearly defining the problems and developing the machinery with which to analyze and deal with them. Unfortunately, the rush to immediate and sporadic temporary solutions characterizes much of our present effort.

Kopper's Company is a member of the producing sector of our economy. Its primary role may be described as extracting raw resources and combining them with labor and technology to create a product that is greater than the value of the sum of the parts. In this process one can see the purest form of the creation of wealth. Natural and raw resources are combined into unique applications that have monetary and social value to customers and society at large. In such an environment, which is characterized by the processing of raw materials and has all of the potential for environmental damage characteristic of such industries, pollution control is simply a fact of life. Pollution control and prevention are necessary, expensive, and ongoing activities at Kopper's. Kopper's employees and management view the social responsibility issue of environmental preservation as being directly relevant to their industry.

However, would corporate involvement in the solution of ghetto housing be as relevant for a company like Kopper's? It is Byrom's position that companies like Kopper's are facing their responsibilities in the area of ecology. In this area, producing companies can bring to bear personnel, technology, and resources to develop and implement control and preventative measures. It is in this type of effort that Byrom feels that his company can make the greatest contribution to improving the quality of American life. He does not feel, however, that it is possible for a company like Kopper's to charge off and solve all the problems of soceity. His firm's philosophy has been to concentrate most on what it can do best. Certainly, Kopper's can and has made progress in the areas of minority employment, community involvement, and other areas where the company is directly affected and can have a direct effect. These activities can be defined as micro in character. These micro activities have focused on clearly defined problems in limited areas. The requisite talent and resources can be brought to bear directly on the situation.

Byrom quarreled with the view that the businessman is typically a schizophrenic. In his view, businessmen do not have one personality and value system at home while carrying another personality and value system to the office. The individual businessman's conscience and system of values is consistant but can be applied most beneficially to the constructive involvement in problems over which the executive has direct knowledge and control.

The greatest progress in business/society interaction will be made as individual businessmen and firms break macro problems into manageable micro size. The business community has not abdicated its responsibility in the social area. It continues to behave responsibly and is increasing both the quantity and quality of its response to social issues. The effectiveness of this response, however, will be directly proportional to improvement of problem definition and analysis and an attack on problems at the micro level.

Banking's Role in Social Action

The next speaker was in an unusual position of visibility in the business world. His organization, the Bank of America, does not specialize in any one area of business activity. Rather, it provides funds and consulting services for a wide variety of business organizations ranging in size from mammoth multinational corporations to small businesses. Chauncey J. Medberry III is president and Chairman of the Board of the Bank of America. Like Fletcher Byrom, his background is filled with professional and personal service to public and philanthropic institutions.

Medberry began his discussion by acknowledging that the challenges to American business are more than abundant. Although there are skeptics and diehards, the majority of businessmen have made the decision to acknowledge and assume a broader range of social responsibility than ever before. Agreeing with Byrom, Medberry acknowledged the breadth of the issue and the problems of the macro approach. The problems and consequences, both foreseen and unforeseen, affect not only the businessman but also society at large. Banking is a unique business activity. While the Bank of America is a large organization, banking by its very nature is community oriented. Each individual branch and its management identifies closely with the prospects and problems of the community it serves.

This characteristic gives banking a particularly direct interest in and influence over many local problems.

A bank's primary responsibility is the acquisition, nurturing and allocation of resources. The major constraint on the banking industry is that the resources and, hence, the power that bankers have is due directly to the funds and good will of its depositors. In addition, the industry is highly regulated and competitive. Considering these constraints, banks do not have complete autonomy. Within their discretionary limits, however, they can and do give major attention to the philosophy and objectives guiding fund allocation. A bank's most direct and efficient method of initiating constructive change is in the development of policies that govern loaning and investing. Some critics have felt that the bank's power over the dollar should lead to a panacea for all social ills. Such critics do not understand the discretionary limits within which banking must work. This is not to say that banking cannot and is not responsive in the use of money and credit to assist in the solution of social problems. As with any single institution, however, its effectiveness is directly related to the skills and experiences unique to its purpose.

Even in the application of its resources to social problems, a bank must be extremely careful. Is it possible to solve the problems of minority businessmen simply by lending them the funds they need to enter business or to enlarge their current operations? This question cannot be considered without giving attention to the rights of the depositors. In some cases, a minority businessman who is incapable of organizing and operating a business successfully can experience greater personal and professional harm due to a business failure than he would have experienced had he not entered into the venture. A bank providing funds without proper analysis of the business risks and without securing the needed counsel and assistance for the prospective borrower may not only lose its money but can also lead the very individual it wants to support to experience an irrevocable failure.

Although the Bank of America is a worldwide organization, it operates in a complex and variable cultural environment. The Bank of America was founded on the philosophical platform of community awareness, service, and constructive use of resources. The majority of the bank's success today is due to the fact that its bank officers have honored the philosophy of the bank's founders. The bank's first general objective is to make available every banking and related financial service that can be provided in a sound, profitable, ethical, and acceptable manner, consistant with the long-term well-being of the community. The other objectives relate to the long-term well-being of those the bank serves.

An Annual Report of the Bank of America summarized the bank's philosophy of operation. The first principle in this philosophical structure is related to the bank's evaluation of a service and its value to the community. This principle requires that a bank's accounting system must include an appraisal of the health of the community it serves. The second principle is that institutions which will have the greatest future value to society are those which will consider and implement change. A third general principle was a vote of confidence for the market system and the freedeom it provided for individuals in our society. The market is an important social and economic force. But it can and should be improved and perfected to help achieve the social as well as the economic aspirations of our nation. The final principle discussed was that of the relationship between business and government. If socially responsible businessmen and business institutions are to have the widest possible effect on social change, the relationship between business and government must be clearly defined. The goal of such a relationship should be to facilitate the most effective collaboration between these two institutions.

The Bank of America has constantly reevaluated its progress in meeting its social responsibilities. Recently, a top management committee was charged with an evaluation of the bank's progress in this area. The management committee enumerated the problem areas in which the bank could be of greatest assistance. The next task was to establish a priority rating for these problem areas. This effort produced a list of great length covering a wide range of important social problems. Based on the decision of the management committee, the Bank of America focused on four areas. The criteria for selection of these four action areas related to the knowledge, experience, and strength in the Bank of America's area of operational influence that would indicate that the bank's efforts could make a reasonable impact on the problem. Parenthetically, Medberry stated that it was foolish for businessmen or business organizations to pursue situations in areas where little could be accomplished. The philosophy of his institution, and the philosophy he recommends for other businessmen and business organizations, is to exert effort in problem situations where the greatest impact can be made. This philosophy parallels that of Byrom's. Following Byrom's line of reasoning, Medberry defines it as "socially irresponsible" for a firm to talk optimistically about solving problems on which it could have little or no impact. The Bank of America's current list of high priority social problem interest areas includes housing, minorities, the environment, and social unrest.

There is an awareness of the social role of business throughout the country today. Most important, there is general acceptance by business leaders of their social responsibilities. To some extent, this grass-roots movement toward the acceptance of social responsibility is clouded by rhetoric and emotionalism. The issue is confused by the lack of a clear governmental position and the existence of well-defined objectives and national priorities. In addition to some of these elements of confusion there is the question of cost — who pays? Undoubtedly, there will be costs associated with taking corrective and preventive action. The only logical answer is that businesses, society, and government should all be sponsoring programs and sharing costs. Agreeing with Byrom, Medberry noted that the problem on the national scale is the establishment of clearly defined objectives and priorities. Only after the requisite analysis is performed can our society develop a program of action and begin with a logical attack on priority item A, then proceed to priority B, then C, etc.

The best long-run insurance for a stable society in which the quality of life in constantly improving is open access to high quality education and the opportunity for useful employment for all citizens. If we can expand and enhance our ability to provide all citizens with the needed skills and subsequently provide for the application of these skills in the job market the success of other social programs will be greatly enhanced. When one considers the size and scope of the social problems in today's society it is easy to become impatient with the pace of change and improvement. However, progress is being made.

Medberry concluded his remarks by cautioning business to aim at the target. It is academic to debate the question of whether business is going to give of its technology, its people, or its resources in assisting with the solution of social problems. The real question is how does business give these resources so that the inputs produce the needed results. Many businessmen want to help and are committed to help but are still groping to find out how best they can become involved. The best way to proceed is to define those areas in which an organization can make the greatest impact and work constructively for improvement in those specific areas.

How Can Businessmen Help — The Problem of Focus

The final speaker was Mr. Martin Stone, Chairman of the Board of Monogram Industries. Mr. Stone opened his remarks by citing that his company was a beneficiary of the socially responsible philosophy of the Bank of America. He stated that when he took over Monogram Industries some ten years ago the firm was managing to lose large sums of money every year. The Bank of America lent Stone's firm a considerable sum of money to clear its debts and refinance its operations. Stone indicated that today his firm is very successful, so successful in fact that it has now become a major borrower from the Bank of America!

Stone indicated that his remarks would be presented from two points of view: first, what socially responsible activities the firm could engage in within the realm of its own business operations and, second, what action the firm could take on a broad social level. Business has moved quickly to act in this area and future movement will be even more rapid and massive. It is possible and necessary for a firm to engage in constructive and direct action in areas of its own operation. In the environment of the individual firm, costs of socially responsible actions can be estimated, the pricing considerations carefully analyzed, and the effects on competition judged. As technology and methodology improve, positive social action by business will improve in quality and become less expensive. The two areas that are susceptible to rapid and direct improvement as a result of the efforts of an individual firm are minority employment and the problems of pollution.

Stone recounted his experience in being deeply involved with the operational problems of his own corporation. As his firm grew and progressed, it became possible for him gradually to become involved with nonbusiness organizations interested in social problems. His experience as a member of the Urban Coalition gave him a chance to lift his head above the operations of his own organization and gain a deep appreciation of the intensity and importance of social problems facing Southern California and Los Angeles County.

In most cases the problems of minority unemployment are not caused by any technical deficiency or unwillingness to work on the part of the minorities concerned. Rather, the problem is caused by pure prejudice on the part of employers and employees. While it is true that certain minority members may lack the specific qualifications for a position, these problems can quickly be overcome through training. When a firm decides it wants to deal with training minority employees, the evidence indicates that it will. Businessmen can successfully cope with this problem situation; they can do the job at a reasonable cost and at a high level of effectiveness. Racial prejudice often prevents this sort of effort from being initiated. For example, a firm may hire minority members in token clerk-type, white-collar positions. In many instances, however, it is doubtful that these individuals will ever be promoted to a higher level. For example, if a black were nominated for a promotion to sales, many people in the company might say, "What will our customers think if this individual calls on them? What kind of an image will they have of our company?" And so, in a situation where racial prejudice exists not in one firm but in many segments of a firm's market, the probability of a black rising to any more than a token white collar position is extremely low. The same problems exist at the blue collar level. If management is willing to employ minorities on the production line, supervisors and foremen often resist. Even in cases where supervisors and foremen go along with minority employment, other employees may behave in a prejudicial manner, thus discouraging the minority member from taking the position or continuing should he choose to join the firm.

Problems of racial prejudice affect the employment of minorities at both the blue collar and white collar levels and can seriously retard equal opportunity employment policies of top management. What can a business firm do in such a situation? Stone suggests that management must largely ignore the prejudicial attitudes of employees, suppliers, and customers and move on with the decision to train and employ minorities. His experience indicates that once these individuals have been successfully trained and employed, their presence in the organization in both blue and white collar capacities is productive rather than counterproductive.

Social problems within the direct influence of individual business firms can be positively affected by individual action. It is on the macro level that business as a social institution seems at a loss when considering how to become involved. It is not that large business organizations do not want to help but rather that they seem at a loss when it comes to focusing on macro problems. Mr. Stone cited a national Urban Coalition Board meeting which he attended. Included in this gathering were industrial giants like Rockerfeller, Roche, Ford, Kaiser, and others. Stone quoted one member of the board as characterizing the frustration felt by the group when considering social problems on a macro level. This individual stated that the problems were very serious but industry leadership needed the answer to the question "What can we do about it?" This lack of direction reinforced the difficulty of focusing on the macro issues. Concentrated around that table was a good deal of the accumulated business power from our nation's largest and most influential corporations. But still, the same problem reappeared: how to define, rank, and focus on the broader social problems.

The key to developing a solution to this problem may be the development of a better working relationship between business and government. Business cannot and should not proceed in various broad social directions alone in an uncoordinated manner. Attention must be given to the analysis of the most meaningful business and government relationship. Then this powerful coalition can be focused finally on clearly defined problems and proceed in a logical direction. The difficulties in dealing with large-scale problems recently manifested itself at the regional level. A group of influential business executives was assembled in an attempt to develop an approach to the housing problem in Los Angeles County. Considerable activity produced a workable plan, and individual companies were willing to contribute seed money for further project development. However, the project stalled when the needed billions of dollars of financing under some sort of federal program could not be obtained.

In addition, the unemployment problem of Southern California was carefully studied. Stone discussed the Watts situation and lauded Southern California businessmen for their assistance in improving the minority job situation from 1966 to 1968, immediately following the Watts riot. Since 1968, however, this program has slowly atrophied. In addition, the soft condition of the economy has resulted in an environment in Watts which is potentially more explosive than the conditions in 1965. Here again, Los Angeles County businessmen would like to provide jobs but simply cannot if the jobs do not exist. This regional and national macro economic problem is another example of the frustration individual business firms experience in attempting to have an impact on the larger social issues.

Stone feels that individual businessmen can have a direct and major impact in the areas of pollution, minority employment, education, transportation, and police-community relations. What will it take to get more businessmen involved? First of all, we have to develop a system of industry-government coordination that will facilitate the application of resources to the relevant problem areas. Secondly, businessmen must be brought to recognize the direct benefit from their investment in social action. All Southern California businessmen can benefit from a constantly growing, healthy, stable Southern California economy. If individual business firms do not become involved in improving the Southern California situation then, in a very short term, many of them will be directly affected. In the long term, all will be adversely affected. Stone closed by describing businessmen as the "favorite sons of our society" and called for a broad-based commitment to the problems of society on the part of the business community.

Discussion Questions

1. a. Compare and contrast the key similarities and differences in the points of view expressed by the board chairmen.
   b. Where do you agree and/or disagree with the chairmen? Support your position(s).
2. a. What are the most important social roles of business today?
   b. Rank these roles in order of importance.
   c. What criteria have you applied in the definition and ranking in a and b?
3. Some writers have argued that "the business of business is business." This argument implies that profits will produce employment, incomes, and tax revenues that can be applied to social improvement by government and appropriate (nonbusiness) institutions. React.
4. a. To what degree are the administrative skills necessary to diagnose and solve business problems transferable to social problems?

b. Cite an example of a social problem which would be susceptible to approach or solution by business problem-solving methods.

c. Cite an example of a social problem not susceptible to solution by business. What reasons support your example?

5. Select a specific business/society problem such as pollution from manufacturing activities. What percentage of clean-up costs should be paid by business? By society (consumers and government)? Support your position.

6. In dealing with business/society issues, what advantages do you see in the following approaches?
    a. Macro.
    b. Micro.
    c. Combination of a & b.

7. What role should the federal government play in establishing and enforcing social responsibility by business?

8. a. If you had the power to make one major change in each of the following three areas, what changes would you make?
    a. our society.
    b. our government.
    c. our business system.
    d. What would be the likely consequences of your recommendation? How would they improve the present situation?

9. a. What are "Value Systems"? How are they related to the business/society question?
    b. Are American values changing? If so, in what ways?
    c. What are the probable short-run and long-run business consequences of any value changes you have suggested?

10. Assume you are the owner of a business and are faced with a decision that will increase your income but not benefit society.
    a. Do you feel you would recognize or sense this conflict? Why? Why not?
    b. What criteria would you use to evaluate your alternatives and reach a decision?

Suggested Class Projects

1. Organize a panel of three students. Each panel member should develop a definition of the term "Social Responsibility" and "The Social Responsibility of Business." Based on the panel's presentation, the class should develop definitions of these terms.

2. Based upon the definitions adopted by the class, several class members should interview local small businessmen.
    a. Record the differences and similarities in the comments made by your respondents and the representatives of big business featured in the chapter.
    b. Analyze and discuss these similarities and differences. Develop a list of reasons that might explain them.

3. a. Have several class members develop a list of the most important problems facing our society. Order the list from the most to the least pressing problem.
    b. Have other class members develop similarly ordered lists of the problems facing business.

c. Construct a matrix and analyze any common problems, related problems, and conflicts.

d. Attempt to reach consensus concerning the areas of conflict.

4. In a pluralistic society the business firm operates in an environment of many conflicting and complementary forces.

a. Develop a list of the groups and subgroups who are involved with, affected by, or interested in business, e.g., employees, customers, managers, competitors, investors, governments, etc.

b. Selected class members should then develop and present a concise yet in-depth analysis of each interest group.

c. The complementary and conflicting aspects of each group and among groups should be discussed.

d. What conclusions and recommendations follow from this analysis?

5. Prepare a short essay that:

a. Traces the historical development of the American business system from its origins to the present.

b. Attempts to forecast the important changes in business likely to occur during the next 50 years.

6. a. Send a class representative to:

    a sample of local business firms

    the civic, social, political, professional, etc., organizations in your community having a number of business members.

b. Develop a list of activities and projects carried on by these groups that benefit the community's welfare.

c. Schedule a class discussion based on an analysis of what local businessmen are doing or are not doing.

7. Develop a "Community Action Plan" for small business. The plan should contain specific and feasible recommendations which could be implemented by the small businessman. Give primary attention to the development of specific and actionable objectives. Establish priorities. Be specific concerning your plans for implementation. Do not ignore the fixing of responsibility for plan implementation. Also, attempt to estimate costs and sources of needed revenue.

Supplementary Readings

Books

Bowen, Howard R. *Social Responsibility of Businessmen.* New York: Harper, 1953.

Davis, Keith, and Blomstrom, Robert L. *Business, Society, and Environment.* New York: McGraw-Hill, 1971.

Drucker, Peter F. *The Age of Discontinuity: Guidelines to our Changing Societh.* New York: Harper & Row, 1970.

Galbraith, John Kenneth. *The Affluent Society.* Boston: Houghton Mifflin, 1958.

Galbraith, John Kenneth. *The New Industrial State.* Boston: Houghton Mifflin, 1967.

Gist, Ronald R., ed. *Readings: Marketing and Society.* New York: Holt, Rinehart and Winston, 1971.

Jacoby, Neil H. *Corporate Power and Social Responsibility.* New York: Macmillan, 1973.
McGuire, Joseph W. *Business and Society.* New York: McGraw-Hill, 1963.
Smith, George Albert Jr., and Matthew, John Bowers Jr. *Business, Society and the Individual.* Homewood, Ill.: Richard B. Irwin, Inc., 1967.
Steiner, George A. *Business and Society.* New York: Random House, 1971. An excellent, comprehensive bibliography in the business and society topic area appears on pp. 569-593.
Walton, Clarence C., ed. *Business and Social Progress.* New York: Praeger, 1970.

Articles

Albrook, Robert C. "Business Wrestles with its Social Conscience. *Fortune,* August 1968, pp. 89-91, 178.
Boyd, Harper W., and Claycamp, Henry. "Industrial Self-Regulation and the Public Interest." *Michigan Law Review* 64 (1966): 1239-1254.
Claff, Norton. "Corporate Responsibility to the Community." *University of Washington Business Review* 27 (1968): 5-11.
Davis, Keith, "Can Business Afford to Ignore Social Responsibilities?" *California Management Review* 2 (1960): 70-76.
Feldman, Laurence P. "Societal Adaptation: A New Challenge for Marketing." *Journal of Marketing* 35 (1971): 54-60.
Levitt, Theodore. "The Dangers of Social Responsibility." *Harvard Business Review* 36 (1958): 41-50.
Louis, Arthur M. "The View from the Pinnacle: What Business Thinks." *Fortune,* September 1969, p. 92.
Marcus, Stanley. "Who is Responsible?" *Business Horizons* 11 (1968): 23-28.
Taylor, William. "Marketing Changing Social Relationships. *Journal of Marketing* 33 (1969): 3-9.

9
What is the Business of Business?

"Why is it such a chore for me to keep my eye on the ball when trying to begin a chapter such as this? Perhaps it's because it is difficult to see the ball, to know from which direction it is coming, and even to define its probable shape, size, and composition."

In thinking of how best to begin this chapter, I tried several unsatisfactory approaches. Finally, in desperation, I stumbled upon the obvious — confess! The preceding "author's confession" immediately reentered my mind. The confession was contained in a marginal note written to myself after one of several aborted writing attempts. Why is it difficult to study, analyze, think, and write about the role of business? Because of the myriad aspects of the topic and the countless number of perspectives from which it can be viewed.[1]

The Cycle of Controversy

In considering the role(s) of any significant societal institution, limitless possibilities for analysis arise. The following list presents the typical steps of generalization and abstraction characteristic of discussions and controversy concerning business' role in society.

1. Specific situation: controversy concerning the roles and responsibilities of business often begins with the consideration of a highly specific situation, such as whether a producer of children's vitamins should use TV cartoon characters to promote the product.

2. Situational context: the discussion concerning a specific case is broadened to include the general functional activity of which the situation is an instance. The vitamin advertising debate expands into a discussion of vitamin and health aids products advertising in general.

3. Institutional context: now the question of advertising and other promotional business practices is introduced.

4. Interinstitutional context: the discussion broadens to include the relationships between business promotional practices and consumers, the government, and society.

5. System context: if not already raised, the question of what kind of economic system is "best" may enter the debate. The competitive market

---

[1] This chapter title was suggested by a classic article in the literature of business: "The Business of Business is...?" by Reavis Cox, *Wall Street Journal*, October 15, 1969.

system, a feature of our economy, is analyzed, attacked, defended, and/or compared to alternatives.

6. Value context: the questions of what economic system is best, how our present system should be regulated, etc., are now debated in light of what the discussants feel is "right," what "should be," and what really is "important" to man.

7. Philosophical context: ultimately, philosophical questions are raised. What is man's purpose? What is life's purpose? What is?

8. Closure and conclusion: this reasoning "loop" may or may not then be closed to complete the cycle. The debate may pass through all seven levels, return to the specific situation, and reach a conclusion and/or a compromise. On the other hand, frustration may result at any point causing those involved to retreat behind the bastions of their positions. The loop remains open, the issue(s) unresolved.

It is the author's hypothesis that more often than not resolution takes place by "closing the loop" somewhere below the level of the philosophical context and the value context. Specific results such as changes in the system, institutional relationships, business promotional practices, a specific firm's advertising, or an advertising campaign for an individual product certainly reflect value and philosophical inputs. Due to their abstract nature and affective dimensions, however, clear thinking and communication at the value and philosophical levels are extremely difficult.

Criticism of Business — Inevitable and Desirable

Any institution that possesses power, has a broad base of social interaction, and is clearly visible to society can count on receiving its share of criticism. During recent times the church, public schools, government (at all levels), education, the military, the scientific community, the medical and legal professions, and business have been the targets of critics. The targets of these social critiques have sometimes reacted with shock and bitterness to the process of criticism. Certainly no individual, group, or institution enjoys being criticized. And yet, the right of each of us to voice our views and to fight for what we believe to be just is one of the things our society is all about.

Society's institutions should expect to be criticized. Business is no exception. One principle of our democratic process is often overlooked by business critics and by business itself. That principle is that the majority rules. The word majority gives birth to its opposite, the minority. If a majority supports a social institution then, by definition, there will likely be a minority critical of the same institution. Business, like all other major social institutions, can not, and some hold should not, please everyone. The supportive majority accepts present institutions and directs its energies toward constructive refinement and reform rather than toward the institution's destruction. This type of criticism benefits the institution. The constructive critic/reformer presses for adaptive change within the existing system. The method is evolutionary. In contrast, there may exist certain subsets of the nonsupportive minority who see themselves as being rejected by the system, or wanting no part of it, and who seek to destroy it. Their method is revolutionary.

Business Criticism in Perspective

Business critics have been heard from for centuries. In the late nineteenth and early twentieth centuries business, particularly big business, was accused of a wide range of socially undesirable practices. These included monopolistic pricing, employee abuse, exploitation of child labor, false advertising, unsafe and unsanitary products, collusion with government, and restraint of competition. The era of the "Robber Baron" resulted in popular and political opposition and the passage of federal antitrust legislation. As the base of economic prosperity broadened in the early twentieth century business became a more popular institution. The failure of the stock market, bank closings, and the severe economic depression of the 1930s renewed the vigor and power of business critics.

In the 1940s the Second World War called for an immediate and difficult response to the challenge and scope of defense production. Business responded quickly and well, serving society and having a major impact on the Allied victory. After the war, business moved swiftly into the conversion to a consumer economy. Since the mid 1950s, business has once again become a target of critics. The following general reasons have had a good deal to do with a refocusing of the critical spotlight on business.

1. The civil rights movement.
2. Increased sensitivity to ecological concerns.
3. Business' logistical role in the Vietnam war.
4. Consumer activism.
5. Political activities including alleged campaign contribution irregularities and influence peddling.
6. The energy crisis.

Business Critics

Neil Jacoby has analyzed and synthesized the general types of corporate critics. Jacoby's typology of corporate criticism "suggest(s) a grouping of business critics into three categories, according to the depth of their criticism and the radicalism of their proposed reforms of the system."[2]

Level 1. The Reformist Critics — "...who accept the basic institutional framework of the contemporary American economy and society."[3]

Reformist critics accept the basic constitutional design of a democratic society and a market-based competitive economic system. Individual freedom and private property rights are supported. The reformist does not want to severely change the business system or the principles on which it was founded. Rather, the reformist seeks to "reform" or "reshape" the system, making it more responsive to contemporary conditions. The reformist seeks to adjust and fine tune the business mechanism. Jacoby indentifies consumerists, environmentalists, antiracists, and others as reformist critics.

Level 2. The Leftist Critics — "...seek to substitute authoritarian Socialism for the capitalistic system of competitive private enterprise."[4]

Among this group are found the socialists and Communists.

An "economic system" may be defined as the way in which a society decided to allocate resources among competing demands. In a free economy, the market system, i.e., the interaction of buyer and seller, determines what will be produced, in what quantity, and at what price. Communist economics feature "state" owned and controlled production and government determination of what will be produced and sold, when, in what quantity, and at what prices. Leftist critics vary in their intensity and in the degree to which they would substitute government control for market control. Leftist methods and objectives may vary from peaceful demonstration and political activity to militant support of violent efforts to overthrow and destroy the present political and economic system.

Level 3. The Utopian Critics — "...reject both capitalism and authoritarian socialism, and seek to establish new social orders based upon different human values."[5]

These critics believe that the basic individualistic (selfish) nature of man can be changed. Again, Utopians differ in the depth and intensity of their philosophy and methods. The "hippies" are nonviolent. They stress passive anarchism. They withdraw from a system they feel they can't change, and they develop their own miniaturized social orders. The "Yippies" seek destruction of the present social order. Their plan for a new social order appears vague, but tearing the system down is seen as the first necessary step in building a "new" system. Humanistic Marxists appear to

---

[2]Neil H. Jacoby, "Corporate Power and Social Responsibility — A Blueprint for the Future" (New York: Macmillan Publishing Co., Inc., 1973), pp. 7-10.

[3]Jacoby, p. 7.   [4]Jacoby, p. 6.   [5]Jacoby, p. 8.

believe that the authoritarian power of a Communist state can be made to function by the substitution of democratic processes and moral incentives for authoritarian penalties. Jacoby cites experiments in Humanistic Marxism in both Yugoslavia and Chile.[6]

The Democratic Paradox

The result of roughly 200 years of free market operation in the United States has been a dominance of many industries by a small number of leading firms. Thus economic freedom has resulted in an inevitable reduction in freedom for some competitors. This paradox of the democratic political system is evidenced by the gradual emergence of only two major political parties. Certainly, each of us is free to run for president, but without the support of one of the two major parties would we have an equal chance of being elected? Certainly each of us is free to go into the automobile manufacturing business, but what are our chances of success if we have to compete with Ford or General Motors?

Is this reduction in "freedom" bad or unnatural? On balance, I doubt it. In order to move forward in government, two major parties may be more socially responsive than a Congress composed of 20 splinter groups. If each of us wants or needs transportation, it may be only through the economies of scale made possible by mass production that the price of a new or used car is within our reach. It may take sophisticated, financially solvent, economically strong organizations to produce nuclear reactors, turbine generators, jet aircraft, or computers. As a society, we have already agreed to grant certain monopoly rights to producers of electricity and water and to airlines, railroads, trucking, broadcasting, shipping, and communications systems. Our reasoning has been that there are advantages to economies of scale, uniformity in pricing, certainty of supply, and public input to operational practices that offset the so-called loss of freedom caused by the granting quasi-monopoly power.

Reformist critics in particular appear to mirror an understanding of the realities inherent in the democratic paradox. They recognize the benefits to society resulting from the successful larger business organization. They also recognize potential or actual instances of abuse of the power held by certain business firms. The reformist seeks to adjust the machinery of our business system making the system more responsive to social needs while at the same time "not throwing out the baby with the bath water." In a pluralistic society, reformists are inevitable and desirable. Institutional

---

[6]Martin Bronfenbrenner's article, "Radical Economics in America, A 1970 Survey," *Journal of Economic Literature*, Vol 8, No. 3 (Sept., 1970), is cited as being the source for the subclassification of Utopians.

inertia may require that outside forces pull and push on the institutional mass resulting in changes in direction as society changes over time.

Thesis of the Corporate Critics

Jacoby identifies five major theses of corporate critics:
Big business corporations are alleged to:
1. exercise concentrated economic power contrary to the public interest.
2. exercise concentrated political power contrary to the public interest.
3. be controlled by a self-perpetuating, irresponsible "power elite."
4. exploit and dehumanize workers and consumers.
5. degrade the environment and quality of life.[7]

In response to these critical themes, it should be noted that business power does not exist in a vacuum. In our plurastic society, each major power source is checked by a countervailing power. Business actions and options are often offset and/or cancelled by one, all, or any combination of the following.
1. government
2. labor
3. competition
4. investors
5. human values
6. resource constraints
7. consumers
8. special interest groups
9. economic conditions
10. internal management conflict

The Tip of the Iceberg?

Your attention has been focused throughout this book on the large business organization and its interface with society. Certainly the wealth, size, and sophistication of leading mass producers and service industries place them in the spotlight. The majority of contacts with business, however, occur between individuals and small business firms. Consider the following:

> In the manufacturing industries, only slightly more than 1/10 of 1 percent of the total number of firms employ more than 2,500 people. Of all manufacturing establishments, 89 percent employ fewer than 100 people and 65 percent have fewer than 20 employees. The employment-size proportions are even greater in nonmanufacturing industries. Of the total number of business firms of all kinds, it is estimated that 98 percent employ fewer than 50

---

[7]Jacoby, p. 10. Each thesis is discussed in detail, pp. 10-15.

people! In other words, most American businesses are small, independently owned and operated establishments.[8]

Is then "big" business merely the tip of the iceberg? Not really. There are sufficient differences between the operations and social power of large corporations and small businesses to warrant their separation for analytical purposes. But, it is important for you to remember that small business activity has a significant impact on social attitudes toward business in general. An unsatisfactory relationship with a small business organization may result in a temporary or permanent stereotype reaction that "business is bad." It "logically" follows that if small business is bad, big business is worse! It is beyond the scope of this book to consider the small business/society interface. This should not imply that this interface is not an important part of the topic area.

Criteria for Evaluation of Business

Jacoby proposes that: "...the performance of corporate business be judged by the degree to which it has fostered progress toward the consensual goals of the American people."[9]

This succinct recommendation is congruent with our democratic ideals. And yet it is doubtful that this recommendation can be implemented. Why? Have you recently seen a written list of the consensual goals of the American people?

President Eisenhower and his Council of Economic Advisors addressed themselves to developing goals for the nation as a whole. Included in these goals were statements related to economic welfare, including objectives of full employment and minimum inflation. President Kennedy also specified national goals, particularly in the areas of civil rights and space exploration, but it is doubtful that these goals were specific enough in the area of business sector performance to serve as evaluative criteria.

The following formula illustrates the importance of clearly defined, widely communicated, and generally accepted objectives (goals) for business as a prerequisite to effective critique:

$C_E = f(OD) \dfrac{P}{a}$ where C_E = potential effectiveness of criticism

OD = objective definition

P = societal population affected

a = the number of the population (p) accepting the defined objectives

[8]Clifford M. Baumback, Kenneth Lawyer, and Pearce, C. Kelley *How to Organize and Operate a Small Business*, 5th ed. (Englewood Cliffs, N.J.: Prentice-Hall, Inc., 1973), p. 3.
[9]Jacoby, p. 15.

Simply stated, the effectiveness of criticism is a function of the ability to clearly define the objectives of that which is being evaluated multiplied by the acceptance ratio, the number of people in the affected population who accept the goals as a percentage of the entire affected population.

There are many confounding variables to this perhaps oversimplified formula. For example, if objectives are not clearly defined, the multiplicative result of the formula is zero. Such a result yields little progress. If objectives are clearly defined but are not accepted, again, the result is zero. It is more likely, however, that some compromise may be possible. In that event the willingness of the participants to modify objectives is an important factor.

However you might choose to analyze Jacoby's recommendation and your author's formula, the major problem remains — what are or what should be the objectives of business? What relationship should business objectives bear to the objectives of other institutions and to our national objectives? Why has our society (as well as other societies) appeared to fail in developing and integrating its objectives? For one thing, objective formulation is an extremely difficult process. Have you, the one person who is more interested in yourself than any other, clearly defined your objectives in all major areas of your life?

> In assessing business performance, we must keep in mind that ours is a pluralistic society. Indeed, the maintenance of pluralism by the diffusion of power among diverse institutions is itself a national goal. In such a society, each institution tends to specialize in the performance of those tasks in which it has a comparative advantage. The society is a highly complex system of interacting sub-systems and institutions, in which the performance of each is affected by that of others. Hence, the business corporation should be assessed primarily with reference to the performance of its unique function of production, taking into account the effects of other institutions as governments and labor unions, upon its performance; no institution in a pluralistic society should be evaluated in isolation.[10]

What Then is "The Business of Business"?

As you reflect on this question you may find it useful to review the comments of Byron, Medberry, and Stone in chapter 8. Consider also the thoughts of Reavis Cox:

> If we think of the Businessman's social responsibility in the sociological sense of being the role he plays in our society, the nature of that responsibility becomes quite clear. He is supposed to keep operating effectively the intricate mechanism by which man's material needs are met.
>
> If he is in steel, his function is to make steel as efficiently as he can in the amounts and varieties needed. As a trucker he is supposed to move goods

[10]Jacoby, pp. 16-17.

from places where they are not wanted to places where they are wanted, again as efficiently as possible. When he operates a retail store his function is to make a wide assortment of products accessible physically at a minimal cost to consumers who want them.

If he fails in these sometimes simple, sometimes intricate and difficult tasks, no matter how deficient they may be in glamor and sense of mission, everything else collapses. So he had better make sure that, no matter what other tasks he may undertake on the assumption that they are part of his responsibility, these basic chores are performed. For here is where his true social responsibility lies.[11]

Cox advises that the business of business is business. He feels that social action by business should be limited to those areas where the businessman has a logical relationship and the capability for producing meaningful results. He leaves the businessman with the following advice:

It also will be well for businessmen to remember that those who deal with social problems must resolve conflicts that often are quite different in nature from the ones they resolve in business. In business, conflict is most likely to grow out of rivalry for money and the benefits, tangible or intangible, that flow from having it. Problems of social responsibility also often have implications for the allocation of income and wealth; but at base they are more likely to grow out of conflicts between value systems. Only secondarily do they become questions as to who is to get what from whom. [12]

What is the business of business? That's a decision for *you* to make.

Discussion Questions

1. a. Refer to the "Cycle of Controversy."
   b. Why do discussion of business and society seem to go from the particular to the general?
2. a. What are your ideas for improving the efficiency of debates relating to questions such as "what is the business of business?"
   b. Should we be concerned about "efficiency" in debate of this type? Why? Why not?
3. a. Do you agree that "criticism of business is inevitable and desirable"? Why? Why not?
   b. How do you like being criticized by family, friends, employer, regulatory officials, teachers, etc.?
   c. How do you typically react to criticism?
4. Do you favor evolutionary change in business and other of society's institutions or revolutionary change? Support your reasoning.
5. This book lists several reasons for a rekindling an interest in business reform.
   a. In what specific ways have companies been impacted by these factors?

[11]Cox.   [12]Cox.

b. Can you think of instances where business has changed or has been changes by these factors?

6. a. Are you a critic of business?

b. Where do you place yourself on Jacoby's scale? Reformist? Leftist? Utopian?

c. How do you react to those on other levels?

7. Relative to the "Democratic Paradox":

a. Is "equality" possible? Desirable? Support your position.

b. Can such a thing as a "free" economic system exist in a large and specialized society?

c. Why are some firms and industries given monopoly power? Is this good or bad?

8. Relative to the five theses of corporate critics:

a. Has society taken steps to offset any of the abuses cited?

b. What pluralistic forces within the firm and society in general act as countervailing forces against business abuses?

c. Are these countervailing forces effective?

d. Should their power be increased? Decreased?

9. In your opinion does the small business firm have any significant impact on society's attitudes toward business?

10. Jacoby proposes that "... the performance of corporate business be judged by the degree to which it has fostered progress toward the consensual goals of the American people." What are the strong and weak points associated with this recommendation?

11. a. If, as the "CE" formula suggests, objective definition is critical to the process of evaluation and critique, why has so little attention been given to this activity?

b. What recommendation do you have for remedying our poor performance regarding the development of objectives for our business system?

12. Comment on these quotes:

"Lack of consensual agreement on objectives means our society has achieved its objective of freedom and diversity."

"The first quote is a cop-out. In order to make progress and continue productive development society must make decisions and take action on a "majority rules" basis.

Suggested Class Projects

1. You have had an opportunity to consider several viewpoints concerning what business social responsibility should be and what should be the business of business.

a. Summarize each point of view presented in chapters 9 and 10.

b. From outside sources bring in several statements of opinion which differ from those in "a."

c. Synthesize and summarize the views you have collected based on their common characteristics.

d. Organize a panel presentation in which each panel member spends five minutes presenting a particular point of view.

e. Allow time for discussion; then have the audience vote on which view they favor.

2. a. Choose a recent presidential administration over the last decade.

b. Through research attempt to locate statements by high level presidential, cabinet, agency chiefs, etc., which embody or imply the objectives of our nation.

c. Attempt to synthesize these statements and produce your group's interpretation of our nation's goals.

3. a. Arrange a debate featuring colleagues or outside guests with known opposing views concerning the business of business.

b. Tape record the proceedings.

c. Carefully analyze the content of the debate utilizing the "cycle of controversy" model discussed early in this chapter.

d. Based on your analysis, attempt to draw a schematic model of the path the debate took.

e. In what directions did the debate tend? Was complete closure ever reached? Partial closure?

4. a. Locate a book, article, or speech representative of each of Jacoby's three levels of corporate critics.

b. Compare and contrast each type of critics's views.

c. Prepare a statement and support of your own position on Jacoby's scale.

5. Is business changing?

a. Prepare a paper addressing this topic.

b. Be certain to compare business practices from the industrial revolution to the current day.

c. Wherever possible indicate the causative factors associated with change.

d. Project your findings into the future. How will business change from 1975 to 2000?

Supplementary Readings

(See also Supplementary Readings, Chapter 8)

Books

Anthony, William P.; Haymer, Joel B.; and Wilkens, Paul L. *The Social Responsibility of Business*. Morristown, N.J.: General Learning Press, 1973.

Evans, William D., and Wagley, Robert A. *Business and Society*. Morristown, N.J.: General Learning Press, n.d.

Hoffman, Abbie. *Revolution for the Hell of It*. New York, Dial, 1968.

Jacoby, Neil H. *Corporate Power and Social Responsibility*. New York: Macmillan, 1973.

Michelman, Irving. *Business at Bay: Critics and Heretics of American Business*. Clifton, N.J.: Augustus M. Kelley, Publishers, 1969.

Reich, Charles, A. *The Greening of America*. New York: Random House, 1970.

Tanenbaum, Frank. *The Balance of Power in Society*. New York: Macmillan, 1969.

Articles

Cox, Reavis. "The Business of Business is...?" *Wall Street Journal,* October 15, 1969.

Davis, Keith. "Understanding the Social Responsibility Puzzle." *Business Horizons,* Winter 1967.

Hook, Sidney. "Bread, Freedom, and Businessmen." *Fortune*, September 1951.
"How Youth is Rejoining the Business World." *Fortune*, January 1969.
Lorig, Arthur N. "Where Do Corporate Responsibilities Really Lie?" *Business Horizons*, Spring 1967.
"Stiffer Rules for Business Ethics." *Business Week*, March 30, 1974. A special *Business Week* supplement.

10

Society and Business – What Does the Future Hold?

The purpose of a business organization of the twenty-first century will not represent a revolutionary departure from the purpose of the business organization of today. True, there will be new technology, methods of operation, and a different business environment. The basic purpose of business will still exist in fact. Business will be expected to maximize economic values by providing income for its investors, managers, employees, and government. Business will, in the main, be looked to for satisfaction of material and psychological needs through the production and distribution of products and services. Certain business critics may be dismayed by such a forecast. And yet, the leftists and utopians only need to look to the business sectors of the ancient world, Hitler's Germany, Communist Russia and China, or a "hippie" commune. Regardless of the political or economic model adopted by a society, someone must look after the production of goods and services deemed desirable by a society. Once a society evolves beyond the foraging stage, tasks are usually divided and assigned to a specific individual, group, or institution.

While the central role of business will not change, and indeed cannot if business continues to operate in a market-based economy, the ways in which business operates will be substantially modified. These modifications will come from two types of pressures, direct and indirect. Direct pressures are those developed and purposely focused on business by pluralistic pressure groups. Indirect pressures emanate from the evolution of society in general. Indirect pressures affect not only business and all other institutions but the lives of individuals as well.

**Direct Pressures — Largely Due to Increase
in Pluralistic Group Activity**

1. Special Interest Groups: groups such as women's liberationists, racial and religious minorities, the more radical left, the Yippies, the S.L.A., etc., will continue to select the corporation as a highly impersonal target for social pressures.

2. International Affiliates: few people outside the field of business

realize the dependency of U.S. business on foreign customers and suppliers. International affiliates have begun to recognize and use their pluralistic power in their roles both as consumer and supplier. The Russian "wheat deal" and the Arab "oil embargo" of the 1970s are excellent cases in point.

3. Professional Affiliates: greater visability and interest in business practices will cause attorneys and public accountants to be more cautious in their approval of business tactics. Academicians in schools of business administration and in the arts and sciences will study and critique business practices more carefully. Academic findings will often be published, further sensitizing potential business critics.

4. Consumers: currently one of the most poorly organized pluralistic pressure groups, consumers will find more coherence through increasing passage of local, state, and federal laws affecting their rights. Even now, a few corporations are beginning to seek ongoing dialogue with consumers by establishing departments of consumer affairs and appointing top corporate executives to formulate and coordinate consumer policies.[1]

5. Labor: organized labor's strength in heavy manufacturing and the trades will continue. Union management will become more professional and sophisticated. Of greater potential impact will be further union inroads in retailing, education, and public institutions.

6. Ecologists: thought at first to be a splinter group enjoying a social fad, the ecological movement has proven itself to be much more. The ecological aspects of decisions are being analyzed at all levels in the public and private, profit and nonprofit sectors of our society. As population and production continue to expand, ecologists find even more urgent fuel to fire their efforts.

7. Investors: it has been estimated that 26 million Americans have some form of stock ownership interest. The majority of their investments are in the business sector. Investor pressure on professional corporate management will multiply as institutional investors, mutual funds, pension trusts, etc., control more and more blocks of corporate voting stock.

8. Governments: federal government activities always make the biggest headlines, but look for increasing business regulatory activity on the part of cities, towns, counties, and states. These local laws will pose increasing future difficulties for business. Current examples are plentiful. In Dade County, Florida, auto mechanics must provide, when requested, a detailed written estimate of auto repair costs. The final bill may not exceed the estimate by more than 10%. The state of Oregon prohibits disposable

---

[1]See Milton Blum, John Stuart, and Edward Wheatley, "Consumer Affairs: Viability of the Corporate Response," *Journal of Marketing* (April 1974):13-19.

beverage containers. Ultimately there will be pressure to standardize commercial regulations at the federal level. The federal government and its scores of regulatory agencies affecting business will seek and obtain additional funding, personnel, and investigative and enforcement power.

9. Internal values: the present generation of young executives and tomorrow's business leaders will press for and achieve more individual freedom, creative input, and a greater balance between humanistic and materialistic values. The ultimate goals of profit and survival will not be supplanted. Rather, the worth and treatment of individuals involved in achieving those goals will increase in importance as business variables.

10. Trade pressures: in the recent past, retailing was somewhat at the mercy of powerful mass producers and most advertisers. That situation is changing and will continue to change. Large chain retailing organizations such as Sears, Allied Stores, and Federated Stores have power of their own now. In cases where a product is unsafe, for example, chains may refuse to stock and sell certain items until the manufacturers make the desired changes. This split in certain sectors of production and distribution will provide a partial system of checks and balances.

Indirect Pressures

You only need look at American society in the nineteenth century and compare it to the current era to assure yourself that the twenty-first century will certainly be different from the twentieth. The volume of change is increasing, and the rate at which change is occurring is also accelerating, much as a snowball rolling downhill gathers both mass and speed. Business is a major societial institution. It exists, by and large, because our society wishes it to exist. It exists because it fulfills some of society's needs. As society changes, so will its needs. As needs change, so will the requirements and expectations imposed on society's institutions. Institutions will change to more completely meet the requirements and expectations of our changing society. These changes will result partially from one or combinations of the following factors of futurity:

1. Urbanization: within the few past generations our urban areas have swollen to accommodate approximately 75% of our population. While urban centralization has produced great economic opportunity for many, it has also resulted in a long list of physical, social, and psychological problems. Urbanization will continue, and all urban institutions, business included, will necessarily be involved in urban problems.

2. Mobility: approximately 20% of our population changes its place of residence each year. As we continue to become a society of specialists and as organizations expand geographically, the mobile characteristics of our

society will intensify. Business contributes in a material way to the need for mobility. Business organizations may be national or international in scope. Special technical or interpersonal skills may be needed at different places at different times. As a firm expands into new territory, people are needed to staff the new unit. An opportunity for rapid avancement may be available to an individual willing to transfer frequently. The personally disruptive aspects of mobility will produce a backlash reaction for some persons while others may be just as willing to move from one location and one company to another.

3. Transience: mobility pressures will make transients of more and more individuals. A transient businessman's only real roots may be the organization. These individuals and their families will look to business to fill the voids left by an absence of family, long time friends, a sense of belonging to a community, state, and region. If increased mobility results in the transient mode for increasing numbers of businessmen and women, internal loyalties will be altered and the current "boss" will be a temporary phenomenon. Long term customers and trade contracts could disappear.

4. The Nonhome: the domicile will lose more of its importance as the center of life. As people devote more time to their work and/or leisure, the "home" will be replaced by the apartment complex, condo, high-rise, townhouse, or residential complex. New forms of ownership and rental will evolve to suit a more fluid life style. Even now, Colorado and Florida condo builders are selling apartments by the week. (In other words, you purchase and own the facility from June 1 through June 7 — forever. Someone else owns the apartment next week.)

5. The Service Economy: within this decade (1970-1980), our economy appears to have shifted from a production economy to a service economy. This means that more of our Gross National Product, the total value of all goods and services produced in this country, is comprised of services than products. This trend will continue. Industries based on service and convenience have burst onto the business scene in your lifetime and have enjoyed phenomenal success. Examples include the fast food industry, day-care centers and schools, rental firms, convenience stores, and travel and lodging industries. Changing consumer needs will provide many opportunities for perceptive (and lucky) firms while others will go bankrupt attempting to sell buggy whips for nuclear autos.

6. The Obsolescence of Knowledge: one government official estimates that by the time a child born in the seventies graduates from college, the amount of knowledge in the world will have quadrupled. No matter what miniscule portion of the world's knowledge the student had learned, he could be considered obsolete by the time he is graduated from college.

Present knowledge is increasing at a rate impossible to match through formal or informal education. What saves us is that knowledge is only part of valued human skills. We also specialize so as to become fairly proficient in at least one area of endeavor. Future pressures to learn and apply the increasing scope of knowledge and technology, along with the potential power of these tools, will be one of our greater problems.

7. The Ripple of Control: as living space contracts, bringing us in closer contact with others, one person's or one organization's activities will ripple out to affect larger and larger numbers of people. Typically we have responded by regulating controls over the behavior of individuals and institutions. A more mobile and transient society will devise systems standardization to provide some stability for the transient citizen whether he is in Seattle in 1980, San Francisco in 1985, or San Antonio in 1990. In a civilized society, laws provide the leveling force of security. Federal control is potentially the more powerful national control mechanism. Federal regulations will continually grow in breadth and depth. Consistent national laws will provide a fluid society with a measure of consistency.

8. Socialistic Drift: socialized medicine, minimum per capita income, government sponsored education, and expanded social welfare programs will move us toward a more socialized society. To test this hypothesis, compare the local, state, and federal social programs of today with those of 1875. Can business remain unchanged by growing tendencies of governmental and public involvement in society's institutions?

9. The Individual: here, paradoxical theses emerge.

Thesis I — The family will erode and permanent relationships disappear.

Thesis II — Mobility and transience will create a stronger need for family roots and basic human value orientation for the individual.

Thesis III — Certainly, future change will occur. However, it will be evolutionary, taking decades or generations. In fact, the process of societal change will never end. Like any other animal, man will adapt to changing conditions. There will always be a minority who cannot accept future change. Some will speak fondly of the "good old days," but life will go on.

Thesis IV — The rate of future change will reach a shrieking crescendo. More and more people will "fly apart at the seams." The cause? Human inability to adjust to a constantly accelerating rate of change. The consequences? A possible breakdown of our society. The outcome? Who knows!

10. The International Dimension: we no longer exist in an isolated world. This country currently carries a mantle of international leadership. Pressures from aggressive opponents will increase. Petitions for assistance from less "developed" nations will increase. Emerging world powers will

complicate our international role. In addition to the probable future changes and complexities, the destiny of our society is becoming inextricably interwoven with the destinies of other societies.

Individual indirect pressures will affect the business sector. Various combinations of future indirect pressures may be even more powerful than the direct pressures discussed. Certainly these future factors are not mutually exclusive or collectively exhaustive. They do, however, present one prospect for the future interface between business and society.

"Future Shock" — Will You Be a Victim or a Beneficiary?

The 1970s have produced two very provocative, perceptive, and readable books concerning the future. The surprising depth of interest in futurism has been convincingly demonstrated as both books climbed to the top of the "best seller" lists. These books did not succeed because they were filled with four-letter words, eroticism, violence, or scandal. Quite to the contrary. Each book, in its own way, addressed deep philosophical issues and changing human values in an intellectual and nonfictional manner. I refer to Charles Reich's *The Greening of America*[2] and Alvin Toffler's *Future Shock*.[3]

You may have already become familiar with Reich's prophecy for the future. In essence, he forsees a new consciousness, "Consciousness III," which will result in a humanistic society in which individual and human values take precedence over organizational and materialistic values.[4] In my opinion, Reich's hypothesis, while attractive, is somewhat utopian. Toffler forsees several specific possibilities, including:

1. Accelerative change which will bring an end to permanence.
2. "Temporariness," transience, and shortened durations for all relationships.
3. Modular man and modular families who will plug out of and into ever-changing situations and locations.
4. Increasing mobility creating modern nomads.
5. Because of the speed of change, organizational forms will shift toward "ad-hocracies."
6. The amount and turnover of information will confuse our internal image building process creating problems of identification with an increasingly complex environment.
7. Scientific advances will provide new human freedom but also raise value issues which deal with the very heart of human existence. Science fiction will become fact. Man's ability to control men and even to create men will confront society with crucial value decisions.

[2]Charles A. Reich, *The Greening of America* (New York: Random House, 1970).

[3]Alvin Toffler, *Future Shock* (New York: Random House, 1970).

[4]For a critique of Reich's hypothesis, see Neil H. Jacoby, *Corporate Power and Social Responsibility* (New York: Macmillan, 1973).

8. Society is currently evolving from the product oriented to the service oriented. Post-service society will feature industries which manufacture simulated experiences. People will collect experiences much as they currently collect "things."

9. For many, the family will become a dead institution. Professional parents, temporary and serial marriages, and scientific fertilization will erode the "mystique of motherhood."

10. Subcults will proliferate. As new values are tried and rejected, people will experiment over time with varied life-styles.

11. A "crack-up" of conventional values will occur. Rapid value fragmentation and turnover will take place, not only in America but in many other societies.

Toffler's far-ranging prophesies will result in adaptability crises for many. The inability of the individual to evolve and adapt at an ever-increasing rate will result in "Future Shock." "We may define future shock as the distress, both physical and psychological, that arises from an overload of the human organism's physical adaptive systems and its decision-making processes. Put more simply, future shock is the human response to over-stimulation."[5]

The remainder of Toffler's work deals with the physical and psychological effects of future shock on the individual and society. Finally, Toffler offers insight into coping with the future and the development of a "strategy of Social Futurism."

Your Future

Consider the predictions of the futurists and the direct and indirect pressures that will certainly modify the future business/society interface as well as society itself. If you doubt the imminence and potential impact of future change, a backward glance of only a few generations or even decades will convince you that your life, as you know it today and visualize it continuing into the future, will be quite different from your expectations. Your work in, interrelationships with, and efforts to influence the business sector will take on new and ever-changing dimensions. The interrelationships between you and all of society's institutions will be modified.

Your ability to adapt to the future has been stressed as a major problem by futurists. In the prologue, I confessed to a major bias and hypothesis: "the individual is everything." Permit me a closing personal challenge along this line. If we continue to permit our institutions to draw control of our society away from the individual, the social futurists will be correct. Our problem will be adapting to a society racing out of effective control. If you, the individual, can reawaken your social awareness and act frequently

[5]Toffler, p. 326.

and forceably having input into what society should be, *you* will determine the future. Society will adapt to man — not man to society.

Our society may have carried the otherwise effective concept of specialization too far. Too many of us have delegated our social responsibilities as human beings and democratic citizens to bureaucratic social institutions. Our lack of time and interest in controlling our own lives results in a disease manifested by the apathetic syndrome. We possess a low resistance threshold to the disease of apathy. Yet, apathy is highly contagious, potentially chronic, and an ultimately terminal infection. The cure can only be administered by each individual — to himself.

Developing and defending your own set of individual and social values will be a never-ending, often frustrating and wearying process. Conflict and controversy in whatever setting will sometimes present you with difficult decisions and personal trauma. Compromise will seldom, if ever, be completely satisfying. And yet the alternative to a rekindling of your individual commitment and involvement may be a society out of control or under the control of whomever might choose to manipulate it. What commitment to the future will you make?

Supplementary Readings

One of Toffler's major contributions is the development of a comprehensive bibliography of source material dealing with the future. The bibliography is lengthy and the sources cited richly varied. You may wish to read in any or all of the topic areas summarized below. Refer to Toffler's book for the detailed listing.

Topic Area	Number of Sources
Individual adaptation	33
Social adaptation	22
Automation	9
Business/economics/consumer patterns	34
Education/youth	17
Family/sex	11
Future studies	57
Individualism	13
Information/knowledge	15
Life styles/subcultures/interpersonal relations	28
Mobility	11
Organization theory	18
Permanence/change	9
Science/technology	43
Social indicators/planning/technological assessment	25
Time	13